RON ARAD:
NO DISCIPLINE

RON ARAD: NO DISCIPLINE

PAOLA ANTONELLI

JONATHAN SAFRAN FOER

MARIE-LAURE JOUSSET

INGEBORG DE ROODE

The Museum of Modern Art, New York

Published in conjunction with the exhibition *Ron Arad: No Discipline*, organized by Paola Antonelli, Senior Curator in the Department of Architecture and Design, The Museum of Modern Art, New York, in collaboration with Marie-Laure Jousset, Curator in the Design Collection, Head of the Design Department, Centre Pompidou, Paris, Musée national d'art moderne/Centre de création industrielle, and Ingeborg de Roode, Curator Industrial Design, Stedelijk Museum, Amsterdam.

Exhibition dates:
Centre Pompidou, Paris: November 20, 2008 – March 16, 2009
The Museum of Modern Art, New York: August 2 – October 19, 2009
Stedelijk Museum, Amsterdam: Fall 2010 – Winter 2011

The exhibition is supported by Notify.

Additional funding is provided by The Contemporary Arts Council of The Museum of Modern Art.

The accompanying publication is made possible by The International Council of The Museum of Modern Art.

Produced in the Department of Publications,
The Museum of Modern Art, New York

Edited by Emily Hall
Translation from Dutch by Beth O'Brien
Interior design by karlssonwilker
Cover design by Beverly Joel, pulp, ink.
Production by Christina Grillo

Printed and bound by CS Graphics Pte Ltd., Singapore

This book is typeset in Replica.
The paper is 140gsm Nordland Woodfree.

Published by The Museum of Modern Art, New York
11 West 53 Street
New York, New York 10019–5497
www.moma.org

Library of Congress Control Number: 2009928917
ISBN: 978–0–87070–759–9

Distributed in the United States and Canada by D.A.P./Distributed Art Publishers, Inc. 155 Sixth Avenue, 2nd floor, New York, New York 10013
www.artbooks.com

Distributed outside the United States and Canada
by Thames & Hudson Ltd., 181 High Holborn, London WC1V 7QX
www.thamesandhudson.com

Front cover: Ripple Chair. Prototype. 2005 (see page 109)
Back cover: Sketch for *Cage sans frontières* installation at The Museum of Modern Art, New York (2008–9). N.d.

Printed in Singapore

CONTENTS

FOREWORD

With the exhibition *Ron Arad: No Discipline*, The Museum of Modern Art celebrates its commitment not only to design but also to the multidisciplinary ideals that inspired, in 1929, its very foundation. The Museum's interest in modern art's ability to permeate every aspect of life was the basis for including photography, film, architecture, and design, to complete its scope and define its trajectory. MoMA has thus always positioned design at its core, striving with every exhibition and with every acquisition to honor design's quintessential modernity: its ability to model the future.

True to its spirit, the Museum continues to celebrate the art of its own time by responding to contemporary art's explorations with interdisciplinary experiments of its own, even by establishing new departments, like the Department of Media and Performance Art. We have at times suspended definitions in favor of a more fluid outlook on the arts, one based on curatorial collaboration and on devising hybrid expressions not weighed down by disciplinary confines.

Experiments they are, and as such they are bound to pose questions and ignite debates. Ron Arad, with his staunch refusal to be defined solely as a designer, an architect, a craftsman, or an artist, leads us to look at the world of design of the past quarter of a century and to notice how far it has come, to what degree it has broken down walls and recovered its spirit of openness, technical curiosity, and cultural pluralism. His work has been imitated, idolized, and also feverishly discussed and criticized, but never ignored; it represents a new territory whose exploration will require effort, courage, creativity, and a good dose of arrogance. The title of the show, which is at once adolescent in its rebelliousness and deeply mature in its contemporary wisdom, spells out just those characteristics, and opens new doors and builds new bridges for young practitioners and theoreticians.

Glenn D. Lowry
Director
The Museum of Modern Art, New York

PREFACE: THE DESIGNER AS AUTHOR

At the beginning of the 1980s, design's need to break with the disciplinary bound-aries of modernism had grown out of its most heated and rebellious phase and reached a new maturity. Gone were the 1970s attempts to annihilate objects and tear form-and-function tyrants from their pedestals; gone were the efforts to debunk the power of corporations and technocrats by refusing to design anything that could actually be produced and sold; and gone were the activists and thinkers who sided with the people and preached that everyone was a designer. It was time to reclaim the creative role of designers as givers of soul in addition to form, uniquely positioned as they were to break with the past and model the world's future.

Ron Arad—who studied art at the Bezalel Academy in Jerusalem and moved to London in 1973 to attend the hotbed of experimentation that was the Architectural Association—emerged on the other side of the 1970s an unscathed (emboldened, if anything) creative maverick. In 1981, the same year the Memphis group was founded in Milan, he opened One Off, his studio, together with Caroline Thorman. This was also the year in which he designed—almost by chance, according to myth—his legendary Rover Chair. In 1983 One Off became a show-room in the Covent Garden market, a vibrant group of small stores, galleries, and restaurants, in which One Off stood out as a laboratory for design experi-mentation, with Arad showing his work and that of other budding, talented British designers such as Tom Dixon and Danny Lane.

Calling the lab One Off was a statement unto itself. Each object, albeit functional, was treated as a focused experiment in the use of materials, techniques, and process. If the human bodies for which these objects were intended still hovered above as the measures for true design accomplishment, the creative act in itself was unencumbered by definitions. The studio's trust in inspiration—whether it be found in a construction system like Kee Klamps, a car seat, or a volume to be pummeled and sculpted and molded—transcended disciplines.

The relationship between art and design has been carefully examined in terms of the perceived juxtaposition between them. Designers have been accused of borrowing art methods and markets; artists have been accused of cavalier gestures such as adding a bulb to a sculpture and calling the work a lighting fixture. Are art and design both ways to act out ideas, or is art self-expression, while design is inherently driven by consideration of other human beings and their needs? Some critics point to comfort as the distinction between the two; others cite economic considerations, sale price, social relevance. Some simply move between the two spheres by switching the number of end users—from oneself to a few collectors to a wider public to the consumer market. Once upon a not-very-remote time, these two disciplines lived happily together and shared the same conceptual roof with architecture and other forms of cultural production, each informing the others with generosity and benevolence. History is dense with examples of universal donors, the O-positives of creativity—Peter Behrens, Bruno Munari, Vivienne Westwood, Ettore Sottsass—whose curiosity and openness have defied disciplinary confines. Schools, academies, and movements, from the Bauhaus to Black Mountain College, from de Stijl to Radical Design, rejected any hint of hierarchy of creative expression.

In the heated contemporary debate on what distinguishes design from art, and in an art market that has been built around the degrees of separation between them, Arad's spontaneous posture, assumed in the 1980s and never since abandoned, has become a postmodern archetype. He is the unwitting father of what we now call Design Art (a term he is frankly allergic to), of all the six-figure sales of objects too functional to be full-fledged art and too sculptural and expensive to be considered real design. He is also, however, a champion of creative freedom, admired and emulated by many designers, especially now that the production and distribution of artifacts has become so diversified, and the channels for expression so tentacular, that any disciplinary definition is deeply hindering.

No Discipline celebrates Ron Arad's spirit by avoiding any separation between industrial design, one-off pieces, architecture, and architectural installation. Objects are grouped in families whose common blood is a form, a material, a technique, or a structural idea, revealing a conceptual evolution that is still amazingly solid with the designer's beginnings at One Off. As much a creature of habit as a versatile artist, he has formed long-lasting relationships with collaborators (Caroline Thorman is still his partner in the studio, which is now called Ron Arad Associates), manufacturers, galleries, and even materials, and thus has built a firm grounding that will continue to enable him to take even bigger leaps.

Paola Antonelli
Senior Curator
Department of Architecture and Design
The Museum of Modern Art, New York

"I WANT TO MAKE NEW THINGS": INNOVATION IN THE WORK OF RON ARAD

INGEBORG DE ROODE

Is there any contemporary designer for whom the use of new materials and techniques has greater importance than it does for Ron Arad?[1] Is there anyone who invests more in experimentation? Although plenty of designers like to work with all sorts of materials and techniques (German designer Konstantin Grcic, for instance, and the young Dutch designer Bertjan Pot), for Arad the new is an imperative.[2] ("New," along with "different," are among the words he uses most frequently in interviews.) As soon as he comes across a new material or techno-logical innovation, he wants to be among the first—preferably the *very* first— to employ it or at least to invent some design-related use for it. The technology of text-messaging, for example, is employed in the Lolita chandelier, which Arad designed for Swarovski (pages 201–3); a reversing of the age-old camera obscura effect, in which an image is projected from inside a box into space, led to Arad's I.P.C.O. (Inverted Pinhole Camera Obscura) (pages 194–95). And by the time other designers are flocking to a new thing, Arad has already moved on to something else.

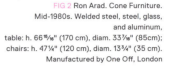

FIG 1 Ron Arad. Round Rail Bed. 1981. Tubular steel frame, structural wire base, and cast-iron Kee Klamp joints, 30¹¹/₁₆" × 55⅛" × 7' 4⅝" (78 × 140 × 220 cm). Edition by One Off, London

FIG 2 Ron Arad. Cone Furniture. Mid-1980s. Welded steel, steel, glass, and aluminum, table: h. 66¹⁵/₁₆" (170 cm), diam. 33⁷/₁₆" (85cm); chairs: h. 47¼" (120 cm), diam. 13¾" (35 cm). Manufactured by One Off, London

In this essay I will explore the significance of Arad's experiments with materials, focusing on the relationships among the unique works, limited editions (or "studio pieces"), and industrial designs, as well as the role of his manufacturers and producers in the process of developing an idea into a finished product. My main examples will be Arad's chairs and sofas, the objects that make up the majority of his work.

A GREAT FONDNESS FOR METAL

The use of metal has been a leitmotif in Arad's oeuvre for nearly three decades. After studying art in Jerusalem and architecture in London, he founded a studio, gallery, and workshop, called One Off, in London in 1981. There he made cabinets, beds, tables, and chairs from unpretentious materials—steel tubing, iron grids, and Kee Klamps (e.g., FIG 1)—with everything designed to the specifications of his clients. He also incorporated readymade materials into his furniture: old car seats, car antennas, and motorbike seats. Recycling was not the point; Arad says, "as a creative person, that is not your main concern. It is someone else's job to consider it." The Rover Chair (pages 26–27), for which he mounted one or two seats from a Rover V8 2L onto a metal frame with Kee Klamps, has become a classic modern design. The chair's character echoes the high-tech buildings being built at that time by such British architects as Norman Foster and Nicholas Grimshaw, but also refers to the materials and forms used by Jean Prouvé, a designer Arad admires, in his furniture from the 1920s.[3]

In the mid-1980s Arad produced a series of chairs and tables in welded steel (FIG 2), a technique that allowed greater freedom than the Kee Klamps.

FIG 3 Images accompanying "The Man Who Collects Chairs," in the December 1985–January 1986 issue of *Blueprint*. Rolf Fehlbaum is at right; at left are his chairs, with Arad's Rover Chair in the lower-right corner.

With their somewhat crude welding, these pieces have a rugged look, much like Arad's Concrete Stereo (pages 30–31), a stereo encased in concrete, and make reference not to high-tech design but to craftsmanship and uniqueness. Few designs in this period were unique objects, despite the studio's name. The majority of work was made to order in unlimited editions, with some pieces produced in a few hundred copies, as with the early Rocking Chair (page 28).

During the 1980s the industrial execution of furniture design was rare in Great Britain. Arad recalls no close collaboration between designers and the industrial sector, although if it had existed he would not have known about it, not being trained as an industrial designer and having no initial interest in the field. The globalization of the design world—now taken for granted—had just begun. And so Arad's first commission came from abroad: Rolf Fehlbaum, chairman of the Swiss furniture company Vitra, asked him to design a piece for the landmark (and ongoing) series Vitra Edition in 1986. Fehlbaum had purchased The Rover Chair for his collection, and in the British magazine *Blueprint*, in an article accompanying photographs of him and the chair, he called Arad "one of Britain's most interesting new designers" (FIG 3).[4] Although Arad did not yet consider himself a designer, his work with Vitra and his presentations at Milan's annual furniture fair brought him squarely into the world of international design.

Despite Vitra's production capabilities, Arad came up with a design for Fehlbaum that he could easily manufacture in his own workshop: an archetypal armchair made from four sheets of tempered steel held together by wing nuts (pages 40–41). The Well Tempered Chair offers an invigorating sitting experience: it appears to be preposterously fragile, but a springy effect makes it quite comfortable—"Soft and strong," Arad confirms, with satisfaction, "like a water bed." More than fifty years earlier, Alvar Aalto used similar forms to try to make his

FIG 4 Alvar Aalto.
Paimio Chair. 1930–32.
Laminated wood and plywood,
25⁹⁄₁₆×23⁵⁄₈×33½"
(65×60×85 cm).
Manufactured by Artek, Finland.
Stedelijk Museum, Amsterdam
FIG 5 | 6 Ron Arad. At Your Own Risk (A.Y.O.R).
1990. Welded, hammered, and patinated
mild steel with lead ballast,
37³⁄₈×21⁵⁄₈×19¹¹⁄₁₆" (95×55×50 cm).
Edition by One Off, London, and The Gallery
Mourmans, The Netherlands.
Private collection, Paris

Paimio Chair comfortable (FIG 4); the elastic qualities of such forms were among the strategies designers began to employ, starting in the 1920s, in order to compensate for the lack of comfort in their unupholstered furniture.[5]

Over the next ten years Arad worked a great deal with tempered steel and continued to use welding. At first, especially in mild steel pieces such as an early Big Easy, the welded seams were clearly visible, creating, in conjunction with the shaping of the steel with rubber hammers, a rugged and craftsmanlike look. As the welding became more precise and professional, the chairs began to look more industrial, with increasingly reflective surfaces creating a dematerializing effect that contradicted their volumes (the Big Easy in fact belonged to a series called Volumes [pages 42–43]). The curved, almost organic forms for which Arad is well known appear in the pieces both of tempered steel and mild steel, more graphically in the former and more sculpturally in the latter, in which sitting often involves a "tumbling" effect provided by weighting the volume with sand or lead—so that the user's counterweight is needed in order to sit down (FIG 5 | FIG 6).

In 1998 Arad began to work with inflated aluminum. He had employed in previous works a technology that used a vacuum process to form parts for the aircraft and automotive industries. During a visit to the factory, Arad discovered that the machinery could be used to inflate aluminum through thick steel stencils, without a mold. The discovery of a new production technique in the aircraft industry is hardly a coincidence; the sector has historically offered a wealth of ideas to furniture designers (including Aalto, who borrowed a gluing technique for strengthening laminated wood in the 1930s, and Charles and Ray Eames, who picked up the idea of bending plywood in various directions during World War II).[6] With this process, he created works completely consistent with his language of forms—for example, the B.O.O.P. (Blown Out Of Proportion) series of large

FIG 7 Ron Arad. Reception
desk at Dolce & Gabbana
headquarters, Milan. 2007.
Inflated aluminum,
43⁵⁄₁₆" × 16' 4⅞" × 23⅝"
(110 × 500 × 60 cm).
Produced by The Gallery
Mourmans, The Netherlands

FIG 8 A Bodyguard is
welded at Ernest Mourmans's
Lanaken workshop.

vases, objects, and tables (pages 120–21) and, more recently, the Blo-Voids (pages 116–17). The parts, inflated in a Worcestershire factory, are welded together with invisible seams, and no two pieces are exactly alike. Thanks to the imprecise nature of inflating into a void, one can no longer tell that different chairs come from the same stencil. One of Arad's occasional larger commissions was a sixteen-foot-long reception desk, made using this technique, for the Milan head-quarters of the fashion house Dolce & Gabbana (FIG 7). Later Arad went back to using molds with Southern Hemisphere (pages 168–69), Afterthought (pages 170–71), and the Bodyguards (FIG 8 | FIG 9> and pages 122–25).

THE PRODUCER AS SPARRING PARTNER

Arad has been working with the Dutch art and design dealer Ernest Mourmans since the B.O.O.P. series, in 1998. Mourmans, who has also produced limited editions of furniture and objects for the Italian designers Gaetano Pesce and Ettore Sottsass, owns galleries in Knokke, Belgium; Maastricht, the Netherlands; and Giswil, Switzerland; and also runs a workshop and exhibition space in Lanaken, Belgium. Since that time Mourmans has either carried out or supervised the production of many of Arad's limited edition series, often the more experimental ones, with other works manufactured in a workshop in Italy, where Arad's studio pieces have been produced since 1994.

Mourmans shares Arad's fascination with new materials and techniques. He also favors pieces that are not easy for others to imitate, such as products made with a rapid-prototyping technique (the high cost of which makes copying prohibitive, but not impossible), which Arad began to use in 1999—probably the

FIG 9 Ron Arad.
Bodyguard no.3. 2007.
Polished and partially
colored superplastic aluminum,
67×33×53"
(170.2×83.8×134.6 cm).
Edition by The Gallery
Mourmans, The Netherlands

FIG 10 Ron Arad. Renderings
for The Original File Was
Destroyed On... (1999).
N.d.

first designer to do so.[7] This process, which fuses particles of polyamide powder into a mass using selective laser sintering (SLS) and a computer-controlled laser, makes it possible to produce very complex shapes. It is a process originally intended for the development of prototypes and models, and in 1999 it was not yet feasible to employ it for the manufacture of large objects, although vase forms and lighting armatures could indeed be made (FIG 10). By the time others began to use this technique, such as the French designer Patrick Jouin, who has been producing furniture with it since 2004, Arad had once again shifted his focus.

He turned to new materials such as a composite of carbon, Nomex, and paper, for his Paperwork Collection (pages 96–97), and silicone, for the Silicone Table and There Is No Solution (pages 112–14); this happened twice at the request of chemical companies looking to display the design potential of new and not-so-new materials. When the British chemical company ICI was looking for a design for Waterlily, a new, environmentally friendly water-blown foam, it approached Arad. The result was the modular sofa Misfits (pages 138–39), which was reissued, made from a different, equally environmentally friendly foam that can be injected into a mold rather than cut, in 2007. Arad's choice of material has been influenced by a material manufacturer only one other time, when DuPont approached him about creating furniture in Corian for an exhibition. This material is a durable, acrylic-based plastic, developed during the 1960s, which was rarely used for furniture or interior accessories. (Such initiatives generate interest in materials, and an increasing number of publications, organizations, and Web sites provide designers with information on the many new materials arriving on the market.[8] Arad seems to make no extensive use of these, yet all sorts of opportunities come his way.) The results of DuPont's request, the Oh-Void 1 and 2 rocking chairs (pages 110–11) and Lo-Rez-Dolores-Tabula-Rasa (pages 198–99),

FIG 11 Ron Arad.
Sketch for Gomli (2008). N.d.

were presented at an exhibition of Arad's work in Milan in 2004. The fluid Corian with which Arad joined the slabs of solid Corian is rendered in a contrasting color, even though DuPont had been proud that the joint could be made invisible.

Together Mourmans and Arad have experimented with the use of silicone in his recent designs, and Mourmans has also played an important role in his current experiments with a machine that produces a seamless carbon fabric (such as for the chaise longue shown in FIG 11)—a machine that Mourmans discovered and told Arad about, knowing he would want to work with it. Mourmans is an interesting creative partner for Arad, largely because he rarely—perhaps never—says that something can't be done, further strengthening Arad's obsessive interest in the new.

This obsession brings to mind the modernist belief, in the first decades of the twentieth century, that new forms rendered in modern materials would contribute to a new social order, and the confidence, during the 1960s, in the sound and inexpensive products created thanks to the development of new plastics. During these periods, materials were often endowed with symbolic meanings, mainly referring to modernity—but such idealism plays no part in Arad's work. His aim, he says, is "to do something. I can't claim I design to save or to improve the world…. Luckily what I do is useful for other people." As such, what Arad represents is a time (the 1980s and '90s) when most utopias had become extinct. He has also said, "I don't believe in any prescriptive theory, in which people tell you how things should be and should not be," and this outlook allows him to remain open to all sorts of developments, so that his work can continue to surprise. All the same, his work, even if not grounded in distinct theories, contributes to our quality of life, to an environment enhanced by interesting, beautiful, and useful objects.

FIG 12 Gio Ponti.
Superleggera. c. 1951.
Ash and woven split cane,
32¹¹/₁₆ × 15¹⁵/₁₆ × 17¹¹/₁₆"
(83 × 40.5 × 45 cm).
Manufactured by Cassina,
Italy. Stedelijk Museum,
Amsterdam

FIG 13 Alberto Meda.
Light Light. 1986.
Composite of Nomex
and carbon,
29¼ × 21¾ × 19½"
(74.3 × 55.2 × 49.5 cm).
Manufactured by Alias, Italy.
Vitra Design Museum,
Weil am Rhein, Germany

TRANSLATIONS: FROM STUDIO PIECE TO INDUSTRIAL PRODUCT

Another characteristic element of Arad's work is the translation of his designs into different materials and modes of production. Arad makes apparently easy transitions from unique pieces and small series to industrial production, and occasionally the reverse, as he did with the MT Rocker Chair, first made in polyethylene as the MT3, and then in stainless steel and bronze (pages 102–3).

Such translation is usually the result of sheer curiosity. In 2002 Arad wondered whether it would be possible to re-create the bouncy effect of the Well Tempered Chair in carbon, a very strong and lightweight material that designers have been experimenting with since the mid-1980s.[9] Carbon is the perfect material to make light furniture—perhaps *the* lightest possible chair, a challenge that has been occupying designers since the 1920s: after the tubular-steel furniture designed between the two World Wars (which was considerably lighter than upholstered nineteenth-century armchairs), Gio Ponti's ash wood Superleggera (FIG 12), and the inflatable furniture of the 1960s and '70s, there was Alberto Meda's Light Light (FIG 13), made of a composite of Nomex and carbon, which at less than three pounds remains among the lightest chairs ever produced. Arad was interested in low-weight materials—as he had demonstrated with the development of his Paperwork Collection and polyamide products—but he wanted to do something different with carbon. The translation of the Well Tempered Chair into carbon proved to be feasible (in the Bad Tempered Chair, page 41), and highlighting carbon's resiliency—in addition to its lightness—was certainly new.

He had also exploited carbon's lightness in a prototype, in 2000, for a folding chair (FIG 14>) with a thickness, when folded, of a third of an inch (a stack

FIG 14 Ron Arad.
Flatpack. Prototype. 2000.
Carbon fabric treated with
epoxy fixative,
open: 31½ × 19 ¹¹/₁₆ × 17 ¹¹/₁₆"
(80 × 50 × 45 cm);
folded: 31½ × 19 ¹¹/₁₆ × ⁵/₁₆"
(80 cm × 50 cm × 8mm).
Prototype by Ron Arad
Associates, London

of two hundred chairs is just over five feet tall). Arad offered the design to various manufacturers, including Vitra and the Italian plastics manufacturer Kartell, but none of them wanted to produce it, not even when the relatively expensive carbon was replaced with plywood, increasing the thickness of the folded chair by only eight-hundredths of an inch.

Most of Arad's industrial products result from his own efforts to find a manufacturer for a design or a manufacturer's consideration of a previously developed prototype or assignment, as was the FPE chair (pages 94–95), which is made by Kartell. This chair, an extruded-aluminum frame that is bent in such a way as to cause its profile to clamp shut around a plastic seat, was originally designed, in plywood and aluminum, for a Mercedes-Benz display, and its ingenious design and inexpensive production illustrates the level of industrial innovation that Arad is capable of. For manufacturers, this is an attractive procedure: when a large part of the design process has already taken place, it is easier to assess whether the final result will be appealing and consistent with a collection.

Arad, as Fehlbaum explains, does not really work on assignment but rather "invents his own brief."[10] If the reality is slightly more complex—Arad does occasionally work on the basis of a request from a client, as he did with the Little Albert (page 105)—the statement comes close to an essential truth: Arad's autonomy is very important to him.[11] Fehlbaum knows this from experience; when he asked for a stackable chair, Arad produced Schizzo (page 82), two chairs that can be pushed together into one. (This is among Arad's few pieces of wooden furniture; on the subject of wood he says, "If you work in wood, then you have to be a craftsman. You need knowledge and experience. I have a different temperament.")

FIG 15 Ron Arad.
Soft Big Easy. 1989.
Metal, foam rubber, and vinyl,
39⅜×48⅞×31½"
(100×123×80 cm).
Edition by One Off, London

FIG 16 (right) Ron Arad.
Rendering for Even the
Odd Balls? Negative
(2008). N.d.

FIG 17 (facing page, left)
Ron Arad. Even the Odd
Balls? Positive. Prototype.
2008–9. Welded stainless
steel, 37⅜×51³⁄₁₆×31½"
(95×130×80 cm).
Prototype by Ron Arad
Associates, London

In 1989 the Italian furniture manufacturer Patrizia Moroso saw Arad's Volumes series at an exhibition in Milan.[12] The series included a Big Easy upholstered in vinyl (FIG 15 and page 43), and Moroso, who specializes in upholstered furniture, believed she could make it better and less expensively. The Soft Big Easy, along with eleven other upholstered models—Arad's first mass-produced collection—were presented by Moroso in spring 1990 (page 50). This collection brought Moroso, who had just started working for her family business, to the forefront of high-end furniture manufacturing.

The different iterations of the Big Easy, starting in 1988, can be seen as a case study in how Arad works. The results of his experiment with carbon were also applied to this model, and, partly owing to Moroso's initiative, a rotation-molded polyethelene version was created in 2003 (page 49). Arad is currently working on a stainless steel variant with an irregular pattern of holes (FIG 16 | FIG 17). In collaboration with The Gallery Mourmans he also produced a series of eighteen hand-painted versions, known as the New Orleans chairs (page 48), using polyester gelcoat to paint the inside of a mold, into which fiberglass-reinforced polyester was then poured, creating on the chair a painting inextricably linked with its construction. The method can be roughly equated with reverse painting on glass, a traditional technique from Eastern Europe, except that with these chairs the painting's support is the last layer applied. Arad first used this technique with the Pic Chairs (pages 90–91), which were smooth versions of the Tom Vac (pages 88–89), an industrial dining room chair manufactured by Vitra.

Arad's most successful industrial product has been the Bookworm (pages 60–63), a flexible bookshelf made by Kartell, which Arad had first produced in a limited edition in metal. During the 1992 furniture show in Milan, Arad invited Claudio Luti, Kartell's senior executive, to take a look at it, and within two years a

FIG 18 (right) Ron Arad.
Sketch of mounting method
used with Bookworm (1994).
N.d.

FIG 19 (far right) Ron Arad.
Reinventing the Wheel (RTW).
2000. Aluminum,
51³⁄₁₆" (130 cm) diam.
Manufactured by Hidden,
The Netherlands.
Stedelijk Museum, Amsterdam

version made from injection-molded PVC was put on the market.[13] Kartell initially thought that the Bookworm's appeal would be limited to publicity for the company, but the shelf has proved to be a commercial success. It is offered in three different lengths (three, five, and eight meters), and to date over fifteen hundred kilometers of it have been sold.[14] In addition to the product typology—a new kind of book-shelf—the most interesting aspect of the design is its ability to be customized, to be, as Gareth Williams has written in *The Furniture Machine*, "personalized in use."[15] The shelf is extremely flexible and can be mounted on a wall, with an invisible attachment method, in almost any configuration (FIG 18).

A limited edition of a rolling bookcase, RTW (Reinventing the Wheel) (page 129), led to an industrial version as well (FIG 19), when Leon van Gerwen, owner of the Dutch company Hidden, asked Arad to design a piece of furniture or an interior accessory in aluminum. The result was this ingenious little bookcase, which can be easily moved by rolling it across the floor, with the bookshelves remaining horizontal all the while. After its promising start, however, Hidden went bankrupt, and only twenty-five of these wonderful objects were made.[16]

THE STRENGTH OF THE FORMS

Arad's fascination with curved, bandlike forms is expressed in both RTW and the Bookworm, and can be seen as early as 1985, in the front leg, seat, and back of his Horns Chair (FIG 20>). Arad's 3 Skin Chair (page 96) makes reference to several historical examples, including a 1947 plywood chair by H. V. Thaden (FIG 21>).[17] Since the nineteenth century, using similar forms, designers have strived to create furniture made from a single sheet of material, which Gerrit Rietveld managed to achieve in

FIG 20 Ron Arad.
Horns Chair. 1985.
Curved aluminum sheeting
and tubular steel,
42 15/16 × 19 11/16 × 18 1/8"
(109×50×46 cm).
Manufactured by One Off,
London. Vitra Design Museum,
Weil am Rhein, Germany

FIG 21 H. V. Thaden.
Experimental Plywood
Recliner. 1947.
Plywood with birch veneer,
upright: 42 15/16 × 19 11/16 × 27 3/16"
(109×50×69 cm);
lowered: 38 9/16 × 19 11/16 × 33 1/16"
(98×50×84 cm).
Manufactured by Thaden
Jordan Furniture
Corporation, U.S.A.

1927 with the Birza Chair (FIG 22>); later they aimed for furniture made from a single sculptural material, which was achieved, during the plastics era, first by Helmut Bätzner, in 1966 (FIG 23>), and a year later by Verner Panton (FIG 24>), who consequently became quite famous for his eponymous chair.[18] Arad used this possibility in a lot of his designs for plastic furniture. The band form comes up again in Arad's experiments at the Vitra Workshop (pages 56–57); in studio pieces such as the Eight by One Chairs and D-Sofa (pages 44–46); and in industrial products such as FPE, the Victoria and Albert sofas (page 104), and the Wavy Chair (pages 107). The much-used form of the reclining figure eight—in the Paperwork armchair, the Corian Oh-Voids (pages 110–11), and the industrially produced Voido (page 118)—is another link to this form, as are the sculpture Evergreen!, in Tokyo (FIG 25> and page 106), and the foyer design of the Tel Aviv Performing Arts Center (FIG 26> and pages 84–85). The decision to use these fluid, often large forms seems related to an interest, perhaps unconscious, in movement and aerodynamics.

It is somewhat astonishing to see how well Arad's designs hold up in various materials and production techniques. Designers dedicated to the functionalist tradition have always maintained that the form, function, material, and technique of a design should all be related to one another, so that one cannot be altered without a thorough reconsideration of all the others. Even in this postmodern age, that idea lingers. So why does Arad's work allow for such flexibility? It has to do with his use of relatively simple forms—the curved band, the fluid sculptural volumes—rooted in an older tradition but implemented in a contemporary manner. These forms are so coherent and have such strong presence, in part because Arad's designs are often produced in a single material and color, that they can withstand mutations of material, technique, scale, or function without losing their value. The sculptural aluminum forms of the B.O.O.P. series, scaled

FIG 22 Gerrit Rietveld. Birza Chair. 1927. Folded fiberboard, 28⅛×29½×24" (71.5×75×61 cm). Stedelijk Museum, Amsterdam

FIG 25 Ron Arad. Evergreen! 2003 Bronze and ivy, 8' 10¹¹⁄₁₆"×19' 9¹³⁄₁₆" ×58¼" (271×604×148 cm) Installation in Roppongi Hills, Tokyo

FIG 23 Helmut Bätzner. Bofinger Chair BA 1171. 1966. Fiberglass-reinforced polyester, 29½×20⅞×20⅞" (75×53×53 cm). Manufactured by Wilhelm Bofinger Production, Germany. Stedelijk Museum, Amsterdam

FIG 24 Verner Panton. Panton Chair. 1959/1968. Baydur foam, 32½×19⅝×21¼" (82.5×49×54 cm). Manufactured by Herman Miller, U.S.A/Vitra, Switzerland. Stedelijk Museum, Amsterdam

FIG 26 Ron Arad. Foyer of Tel Aviv Performing Arts Center. 1988–94

FIG 27 Arad, with
A Suitable Case (1994),
a wooden container for
London Papardelle (1992).
See pages 52–53

down into pressed BabyBoop Bowls (page 120) for Alessi, are still a well-designed product, perhaps one of the few examples of miniaturization leading to a useful object.

This does not mean, however, that Arad's work is solely formalist in character. With few exceptions, function—and this, for Arad, means comfort, particularly in the chairs and sofas—remains essential: "Even when no one will sit on it," he says, "I want to make a chair perfect" (FIG 27). And nearly all of his chairs are indeed very comfortable, even the studio pieces that occasionally look more like nonfunctional objects than furniture.

INFLUENCE

Arad is passing his design approach to future generations of designers through his work and teaching, but his language of forms is probably too personal (or too universal) to gather a following among other designers (one of the few designers who shows an affinity with him in this respect is Marc Newson [FIG 28>], but there seems to be no hint of mutual influence).[19] But because Arad for the most part sets his own course, he encourages openness and autonomy in other designers as well. His most profound influence is in the realm of experimentation with materials and techniques and combinations of the two, in striking designs and spectacular presentations that get the attention of colleagues, producers, and the press. Innovation, then, is his greatest strength, and as his reputation grows, so will his influence.

FIG 28 Marc Newson.
Embryo Chair. 1988.
Chromed steel and
polyurethane foam covered
with bi-elastic fabric,
31½ × 33½ × 31½"
(80 × 85.1 × 80 cm).
The Museum of Modern Art,
New York. Gift of Patricia
Phelps de Cisneros in honor
of Tomás Orinoco
Griffin-Cisneros

[1] The statement in the title is taken from an interview with Ron Arad conducted by the author, May 7, 2008. Unless otherwise noted, all quotes from Arad are taken from this interview. On Arad's interest in making "new things," see also Matthew Collings, *Ron Arad Talks to Matthew Collings* (London: Phaidon, 2004), pp. 202–4. Other sources for this essay were Alexander von Vegesack, *Ron Arad* (Weil am Rhein, Germany: Vitra Design Museum, 1990), Deyan Sudjic, *Ron Arad* (London: Laurence King / Bangert, 1999), and interviews with Ernest Mourmans (May 27, 2008), Rolf Fehlbaum (May 21, 2008), and Patrizia Moroso (May 21–22, 2008).

[2] On Konstantin Grcic and Bertjan Pot, see Florian Böhm, *KGID: Konstantin Grcic Industrial Design* (London: Phaidon, 2005); Mel Byars, *New Chairs: Design, Technology, and Materials* (London: Laurence King, 2006); Ingeborg de Roode, "Bertjan Pot," *Stedelijk Museum Bulletin* 18, no. 1 (2005): 30–32, 56–57; and Gareth Williams, *The Furniture Machine: Furniture since 1990* (London: V&A Publications, 2006).

[3] For a comparison between The Rover Chair and a 1924 prototype by Jean Prouvé, see Charlotte and Peter Fiell, *1000 Chairs* (Cologne: Benedikt Taschen, 2000), p. 562.

[4] Peter Murray, "The Man Who Collects Chairs," *Blueprint*, no. 23 (December 1985–January 1986): 24–26.

[5] On the influence of materials and techniques on furniture design, see Ingeborg de Roode, "150 Years of Furniture Design: Does Form Follow Function?" (working title), forthcoming in *Re-view: New Perspectives on the Stedelijk Museum's Collection* (Amsterdam: Stedelijk Museum and NAi Publishers). On the Paimio Chair, see Derek E. Ostergard, *Bent Wood and Metal Furniture, 1850–1946* (New York: The American Federation of Arts, 1987), pp. 309–10; and Alexander von Vegesack, *100 Masterpieces from the Vitra Design Museum* (Weil am Rhein, Germany: Vitra Design Museum, 1995).

[6] Ostergard, *Bent Wood and Metal Furniture*, pp. 160–69, 325–31, and de Roode, "150 Years of Furniture Design."

[7] Mourmans interview, May 27, 2008. In that same year, for the project *Vaas voor de gelegenheid,* Marcel Wanders designed an object using the SLS technique as well. That project was presented at the end of the year; Arad presented his SLS pieces at the Milan Furniture Fair in April 1999.

[8] Examples include www.materialconnexion.com, a Web site based in New York, and Rotovision's series of books by Chris Lefteri, a designer and teacher at Central Saint Martin's, in London.

[9] Carbon fiber has a soft and fibrous structure and therefore always needs a fixative (usually a synthetic resin) in order to be used in the constructive sense. The term "carbon" usually denotes the material treated with fixative. On the use of carbon in furniture design, see de Roode, "150 Years of Furniture Design."

[10] Fehlbaum interview, May 21, 2008.

[11] Moroso asked him to add a small armchair to the Victoria and Albert Collection, and Little Albert was the result; Moroso interview, May 21–22, 2008.

[12] Ibid.

[13] Arad interview, May 7, 2008, and information provided to the author by Kartell, May 28, 2008. For more about the Bookworm, see Volker Albus, *Design-Klassiker: Der Bookworm von Ron Arad* (Frankfurt am Main: Verlag Form, 1997).

[14] Information provided by Kartell.

[15] Williams, *The Furniture Machine,* p. 118.

[16] Leon van Gerwen, interview with the author, April 5, 2001. Hidden b.v. went bankrupt on May 19, 2004; information provided by 's-Hertogenbosch Chamber of Commerce.

[17] On H. V. Thaden, see von Vegesack, *100 Masterpieces*, p. 116.

[18] On Gerrit Rietveld's Birza Chair, see Marijke Küper and Ida van Zijl, eds., *Gerrit Th. Rietveld: The Complete Works* (Utrecht: Centraal Museum, 1992), p. 115. On Helmut Bätzner, see von Vegesack, *100 Masterpieces*, pp. 46–47. On Verner Panton, see Mathias Remmele, "All of a Piece: The Story of the Panton Chair," in Remmele and von Vegesack, eds., *Verner Panton: The Collected Works* (Weil am Rhein, Germany: Vitra Design Museum, 2000), pp. 74–99.

[19] On Marc Newson, see Conway Lloyd Morgan, *Marc Newson* (New York: Universe Publishing, 2003); and Louise Neri, *Marc Newson* (New York: Gagosian Gallery, 2007).

The Rover Chair. 1981
Tubular steel, leather, and cast-iron Kee Klamp joints
30¾ × 27³⁄₁₆ × 36¼" (78 × 69 × 92 cm)
Edition by One Off, London

<Rover   Moreover∧

The Rover Chair, the launching point for Arad's career, was the first successful design for his studio, One Off, and is emblematic of his early readymade creations. Having completed his studies at the Architectural Association, in London, Arad crossed over into the world of design when, while scavenging in a scrap yard, he was struck by the engineering and craftsmanship of some discarded leather seats from a Rover V8 2L; inspired by their comfort and availability, he bought two (in red, which was later found to be very rare). These he dismantled and anchored in tubular-steel frames using Kee Klamps, an inexpensive scaffolding system invented, in the 1930s, for cow-milking stalls. On Boxing Day in 1981 Arad sold the first two Rover Chairs (unknowingly) to Jean Paul Gaultier, who had knocked on the window of his closed studio.

These chairs soon became hugely popular, but Arad stopped producing them once the supply of usable seats was exhausted. Although he was aware at the time of many illustrious artistic experiments made with found objects, his intention was not to participate in this legacy. Nor, he insists, was recycling, although the Rover has been misinterpreted as an environmental statement. He had not conceived this classic design as a manifesto of any kind. It was simply something he could do that was easy and, above all, different, and it was The Rover Chair that brought Arad into the world of international design. With Moreover, Vitra re-created the original form in limited editions of rust and chrome, creating another ending for the story of the Rover: an industrial creation that no longer relied on salvaged materials.

Sketches for The Rover Chair (1981). N.d. [top & bottom left]

Moreover. 2007
Patinated rusted steel [center] or chromed steel [right]
37⅜ × 29½ × 35¹³⁄₁₆" (95 × 75 × 91 cm)
Edition by Ron Arad Associates, London

^Rocking Chair

The Rocking Chair, lacking the curved feet of
traditional rockers, relies on its name to indicate its
function. Made of bent tubular steel, it creates
a different, somewhat scissorlike rocking movement.
It was this mechanical idea, rather than an aesthetic
quality, that Arad intended as the meaning of the chair,
and he has indeed denied that it is at all stylish.
This chair holds special significance as his first proper
work of design—or, rather, the first time he was aware
that he was designing. It signals his earliest venture
beyond the readymade and toward design that did not
rely on salvaged or repurposed materials. The final
version of the Rocking Chair is sleeker than the original,
which was conceived as another Kee Klamp construction (and determined too risky for unsuspecting
fingers). One Off made several hundred of these chairs.

Rocking Chair. 1981
Tubular steel and PVC plastic–covered galvanized springs
31½ × 23⅝ × 15¾" (80 × 60 × 40 cm)
Edition by One Off, London

Round Rail Bed⌃

Steel tubing, Kee Klamps, and quick drawings were the currency of One Off's early days, when people came to the studio as much to see ideas in physical evolution as actual furniture. The accessible and affordable Kee Klamp system, with its universal and standardized steel tubing and numerous cast iron joints, fueled the creation of flexible, even personalized designs at a reasonable cost; these included many architectural installations, such as storage systems, desks, shelving, and loft beds (a studio mainstay), all with an industrial appearance that fit the high-tech look favored in London at the time. The Round Rail Bed, simply constructed and structurally supported by its wire-mesh base, was inspired by a common industrial shelving called Metro, still sold by Slingsby Industrial and Commercial Equipment. Arad himself still sleeps in one of these beds.

Round Rail Bed. 1981
Tubular steel frame, structural wire base, and cast-iron Kee Klamp joints
30 11/16" × 55 1/8" × 7' 4 5/8" (78 × 140 × 220 cm)
Edition by One Off, London

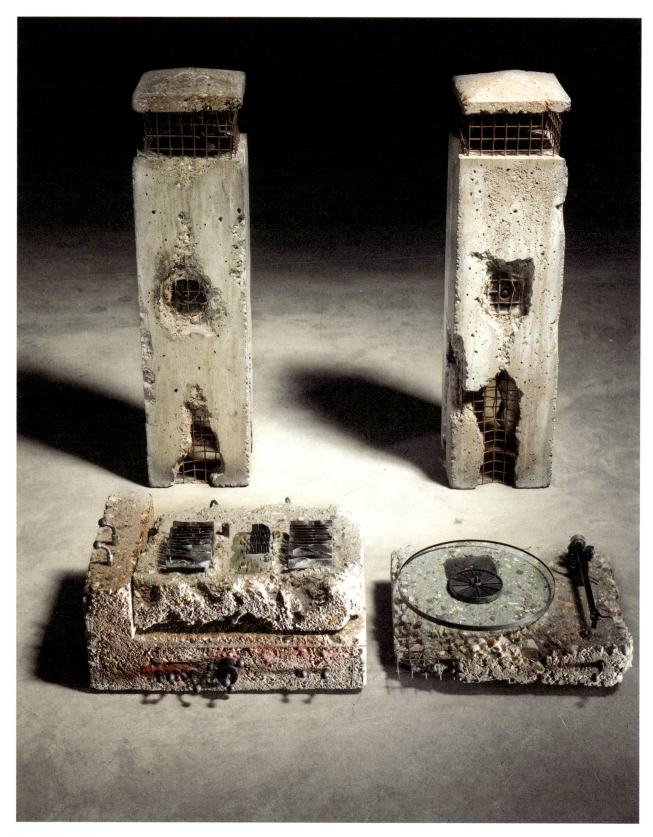

Concrete Stereo. 1983
Turntable, amplifier, two speakers,
and electronic components embedded in concrete
Dimensions variable
Edition by One Off, London

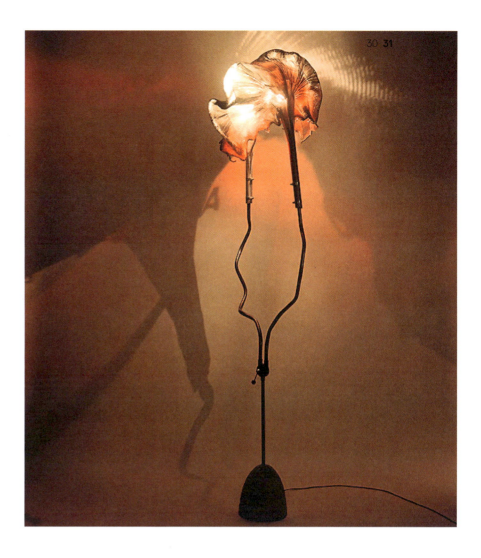

<Concrete Stereo

The Concrete Stereo is another milestone in Arad's work with readymades. A hi-fi range (record player, speakers, and amplifier) was first coated with protective resin and then encased in concrete slabs; soon afterward the concrete was partially chipped away, exposing the rusting steel beneath. At the time of this experiment Arad was interested in both concrete and electronics, and he enjoyed the unfamiliar juxta-position of these components as well as the technique involved in uniting them; he has compared the uncom-fortable combination of materials, both physical and semiotic, to Meret Oppenheim's fur-covered teacup set. The stereo produced something less than high-quality sound—a surreal challenge to the sanctity of consumer electronics. Very few Concrete Stereos were made, but the idea was ripe for imitation, and knockoffs were soon appearing in novelty shops. This cooled Arad's enthusiasm, although he still regards these works as objects of beauty.

Armadillo Light. 1985
Concrete base, flexible steel arms,
aluminum honeycomb shade, and halogen bulb
H. 7' 4⅝" (220 cm), diam. 10⅝" (27 cm)
Edition by One Off, London

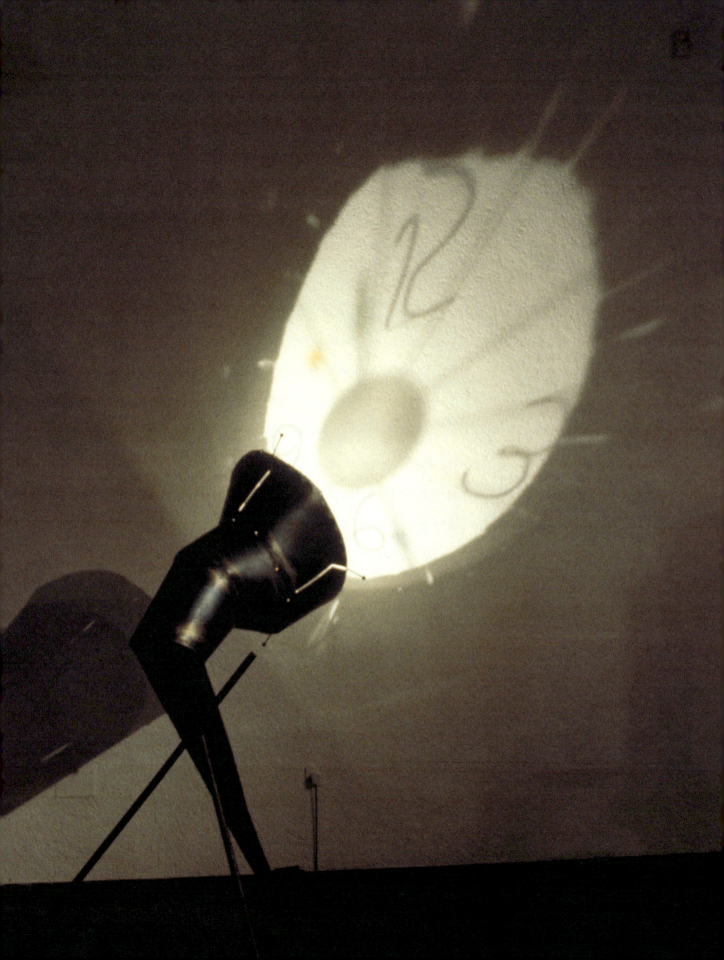

<Shadow of Time

Shadow of Time, one of the highlights of Arad's steel work from the 1980s, is a lamp that projects a working clock face onto a ceiling or wall. Its body is a hollow, jagged horn that rests on two thin legs of a tripod, with the third leg formed by the horn itself. Both the lamp and the shadow it casts are adjustable: the conical steel head pivots 360 degrees; the projection can be focused to keep the numbers sharp; and the halogen light is controlled with a dimmer. Cones and cylinders are volumes commonly found in Arad's early work with sheet steel; the form of this lamp is rooted in the design for a huge conical balustrade for his shop's staircase. The concept for Shadow of Time, which was produced in an edition of twenty, was born when Arad thought he saw a clock projected onto a showroom ceiling, realized he had imagined it, and decided to create one himself.

Aerial Light>

The Aerial Light is another early readymade, one that Arad considers more sophisticated and what Marcel Duchamp would have deemed an "assisted readymade." This lamp, which allows users to change the angle of light with a remote control, is made of a halogen bulb attached to a cable and a telescopic car aerial and connected to an electric motor; the design was developed with help from the Japanese company Nippon Antenna and Peter Keene, a designer in Arad's studio. Fully extended, it is three feet long—Arad has compared it to a remote-controlled fishing rod. Initially the remote control units were connected to the lamp with cables; in a subsequent version they were ultrasonic, and then finally infrared. The lamp is omnidirectional: its angle can be adjusted in three dimensions, an upgrade of the flexibility provided by the classic Anglepoise lamp. The Aerial Light's ad hoc quality is enhanced by the Letraset transfer letters Arad used to spell out the words "patent pending" and by images of his fingerprints adorning the pads used to control the direction of movement. It was this piece that prompted the nickname "Mad Max"—much to Arad's displeasure—after the dystopian Australian film.

Shadow of Time. 1986 [opposite]
Patinated steel, stainless steel, and clock mechanism
H. 70⅞" (180 cm), diam. 19⅝" (50 cm)
Edition by One Off, London

Aerial Light. 1981 [above]
Lacquered steel, cast iron, car aerial, electronic components, and halogen bulb
51³⁄₁₆ × 11¹⁵⁄₁₆ × 8⅝" (130 × 30 × 22 cm)
Edition by One Off, London

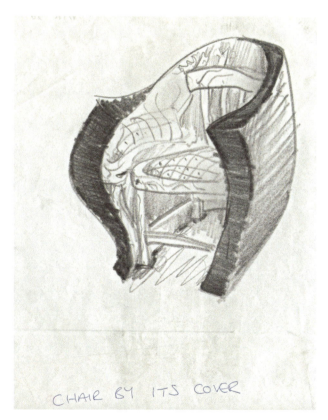

^Chair By Its Cover

Why design a chair when so many already exist? One of these chairs asks as much with its mysterious inscription "Why bark if you can have a dog?" This pair is a monument to the readymade: two unassuming chairs enrobed in gleaming, mirror-polished steel, thus transformed into something massive and powerful. But the second chair, inscribed "Why have a dog if you can bark yourself?" suggests a further thought: Who really needs new chairs after all?

2 R Not>

Unlike most of Arad's metal furniture, 2 R Not is meant to be played with and moved around. It is a bronze or steel cube that can be turned on different sides, so that the single piece is actually several chairs of different heights. The name reveals the simple puzzle of its function: four of the six possible positions are chairs, while two are not.

Chair By Its Cover. 1989 [top left]
Patinated and mirror-polished steel with metal and leather chair
37³⁄₈ × 43⁵⁄₁₆ × 35⁷⁄₁₆" (95 × 110 × 90 cm)
Edition by One Off, London
Sketch for Chair By Its Cover (1989). N.d. [bottom]

Chair By Its Cover. 1989 [top right]
Patinated and mirror-polished steel with wood and leather chair
37³⁄₈ × 43⁵⁄₁₆ × 35⁷⁄₁₆" (95 × 110 × 90 cm)
Edition by One Off, London

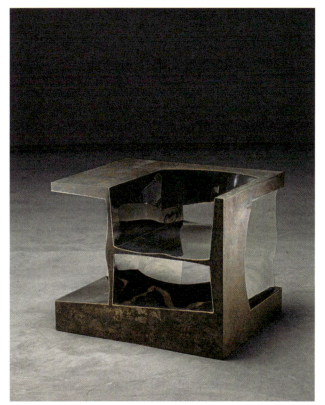

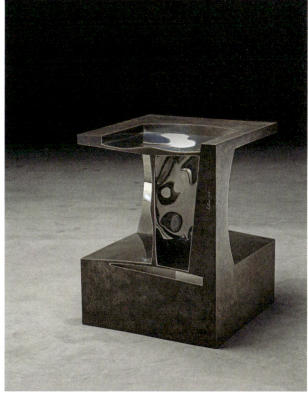

2 R Not. 1992 [top left]
Patinated and mirror-polished bronze
24×30⅛×24" (61×76.5×61 cm)
Edition by Ron Arad Associates, London

2 R Not. 1992 [top right, bottom left & right]
Patinated mild steel and mirror-polished stainless steel
24×30⅛×24" (61×76.5×61 cm)
Edition by Ron Arad Associates, London

Happy Days. 1992
Patinated mild steel and mirror-polished stainless steel
31½ × 51³⁄₁₆ × 29½" (80 × 130 × 75 cm)
Edition by One Off, London

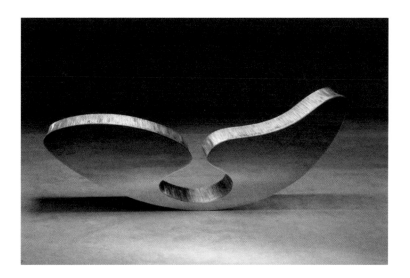

Looploom︿

Looploom combines Arad's love of rocking chairs
and chaise longues — a career-long passion that has
led him to invent new seating archetypes — with his
exploration of the hidden qualities of steel, which in his
hands can become as bouncy as polyurethane foam and
as malleable as a natural fiber. In several pieces from
the early 1990s, including Looploom, Arad used woven
steel stretched over a steel frame like a hammock, rely-
ing on its reaction to the shifting weight of the human
body to keep the seat in tension.

Looploom. 1992
Polished stainless steel mesh and steel
27 9/16" × 7' 2 5/8" × 15 3/4" (70 × 220 × 40 cm)
Edition by One Off / Ron Arad Associates, London

Tinker Chair

The Tinker Chairs are rough forms, hammered by hand, with welded side seams. These abstract, sculptural chairs represent Arad's early, raw relationship with sheet steel, his favorite material, as mediated by a rubber hammer. The process of manufacturing them was improvisational—each of them handmade and tweaked for additional comfort, and each of them unique, marked by unplanned twisting and colors in the metal, from the welding. To Arad, they represent a learning process—"I didn't know any better," he says—revealing what he was able to do at the time.

Tinker Chair. 1988 [left]
Painted and patinated hammered steel
37⅜×19⅝×31½" (95×50×80 cm)
Edition by One Off, London

Tinker Chair. 1988 [right]
Painted and patinated hammered steel
37⅜×17¾×28¾" (95×45×73 cm)
Edition by One Off, London

Sketch for Tinker Chair (1988) **and other objects from the Volumes series** (1986). N.d.

Well Tempered Chair. Prototype. 1986
Sprung stainless steel with wing nuts
31½ × 39⅜ × 31½" (80 × 100 × 80 cm)
Prototype by Vitra GmbH, Germany

<Well and
Bad Tempered Chair ∧

The Well Tempered Chair, Arad's first commission from a major manufacturer, was clearly inspired by the shape of the archetypal plush club chair, the epitome of comfort. Made as it is of cold steel, however, the chair looks forbidding, and yet, in another reversal, it subverts our expectations by proving to be quite comfortable. Its construction—four sheets of steel looped and bolted with wing nuts—is an example of how Arad likes to play and experiment and push a material to its very limits. The chair's name is a play on its execution: tempering is a heat treatment that gives steel memory, allowing it to return to its original shape after being bent or distorted, but "well tempered" also suggests an amiability and sense of humor that contrasts with the

work's rather threatening appearance. The elastic strength of the sheet steel allows it to be curved quite sharply and provides some bounce to the seat, contradicting the sitter's expectation of a hard and ungiving surface. Arad's challenging use of material is paired here with a "what you see is what you get" impression; as Arad has put it, the piece is all skin— no bones, fat, or muscle. In the Bad Tempered Chair, produced in a limited edition of one thousand, this skin is no longer steel but a new type of fiber composite— glass, carbon, and Kevlar fiber laminates embedded in an artificial resin. The simple form and elasticity of the original are preserved in a chair that is also incredibly light.

Bad Tempered Chair. 2002 [left]
Carbon, Kevlar, and glass fiber with wing nuts
29½ × 40 × 32⁵⁄₁₆" (75 × 101.5 × 82 cm)
Manufactured by Vitra GmbH, Germany
Sketch for Well Tempered Chair (1986). N.d. [right]

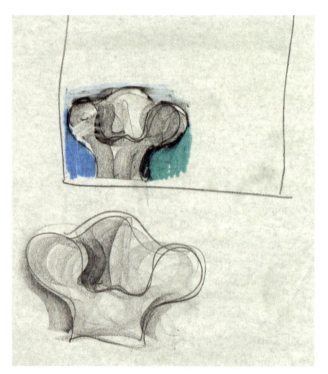

The Volumes

Arad's work with tempered steel, particularly his grasp of the expressive and formal possibilities of welding, matured in the years following the Well Tempered Chair. These changes are apparent in the Big Easy, from his Volumes series: a large, hollow armchair with ballooning arms that blurs the distinction between furniture and sculpture. The earliest Big Easy, made in 1988, was rugged, with visible welded seams holding together its curved steel parts. Later versions were more refined, with their surfaces highly polished to create reflective and distorting effects, and an upholstered version was

Big Easy Volume 2. 1989 [top left]
Stainless steel and antirust paint
39 × 49⅝ × 31½" (99 × 126 × 80 cm)
Edition by One Off/Ron Arad Associates, London

Big Easy Volume 2. 1988 [top right]
Polished stainless steel
42⅛ × 50½ × 36¼" (107 × 128.3 × 92.1 cm)
Edition by One Off, London
Sketches for Big Easy Volume 2 (1988). N.d. [bottom left & right]

made from a slightly smaller steel frame padded with foam. The chair, displayed during the Milan Furniture Fair, caught the eye of Patrizia Moroso, who had just taken over the creative direction of her family's furniture business, and inspired her to commission the Soft Big Easy, taking the form into industrial production. This family of chairs, revived in 1999 with the New Orleans series (page 48), is an outstanding example of how Arad tenaciously and exhaustively reworks his own designs, using different materials, processes, and tones to give full play to his idiosyncratic ideas.

Soft Big Easy. 1990 [top & bottom]
Polyurethane stuffing, wool, and foam
39⅜ × 48⁷⁄₁₆ × 31½" (100 × 123 × 80 cm)
Manufactured by Moroso SpA, Italy

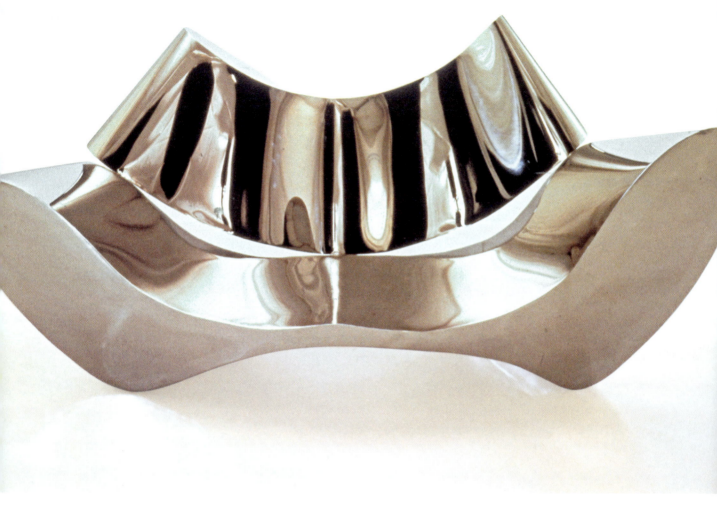

D-Sofa. Prototype. 1994 [previous page]
Patinated, painted, oxidized stainless steel and mild steel
38³⁄₁₆″ × 7′ 1¹⁵⁄₁₆″ × 35⁷⁄₁₆″ (97 × 218 × 90 cm)
Prototype by One Off, London

D-Sofa. 1994 [top]
Mirror-polished stainless steel
38³⁄₁₆″ × 7′ 1¹⁵⁄₁₆″ × 35⁷⁄₁₆″ (97 × 218 × 90 cm)
Edition by One Off, London
Sketch for D-Sofa (1994). N.d. [bottom]

Big Heavy. 1989 [top left]
Patinated mild steel
35 ¹³⁄₁₆ × 31½ × 43" (91 × 80 × 109 cm)
Edition by One Off, London, and The Gallery Mourmans, The Netherlands
Big Heavy. 1989 [bottom left]
Patinated mild steel with polished stainless steel welds
29 × 23 ⅝ × 24 ¹³⁄₁₆" (73.5 × 60 × 63 cm)
Edition by One Off, London, and The Gallery Mourmans, The Netherlands

Sketch for Big Heavy (1989). N.d. [top right]
Little Heavy. 1989 [bottom right]
Polished stainless steel
30 × 25 ⅝ × 27½" (76 × 65 × 70 cm)
Edition by One Off / Ron Arad Associates, London
Sketch for Little Heavy (1989). N.d. [bottom center]

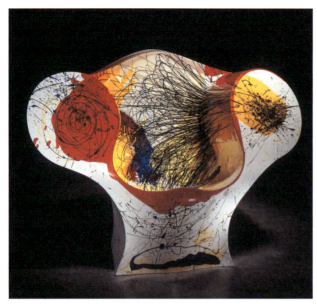

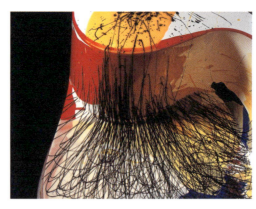

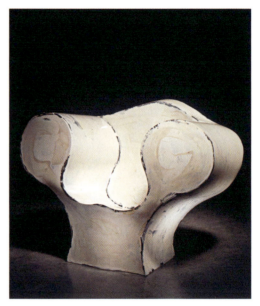

^New Orleans

The New Orleans chairs are an edition of eighteen colorful armchairs made in the same shape as the Big Easy (page 42). Arad made these for The Gallery Mourmans, each one built up from the inside out, in pigmented polyester gelcoat applied in layers and fiberglass-reinforced polyester. He painted the chairs by applying the gelcoat in layers inside the molds before pouring in the polyester, thus making the decorative element inherent to the chair's construction, a method first used with the Pic Chairs (pages 90–91). For these chairs Arad favored bright primary colors in abstract drips and bursts, with the occasional random message, such as "Absolutely not for sale," "No plan just do it," and "The last one was not so very brilliant, this one must be!"

New Orleans. 1999
Fiberglass, polyester, and gelcoat
35 7/8 × 42 × 29 1/8" (91 × 122 × 74 cm)
Edition by Ron Arad for The Gallery Mourmans, The Netherlands

The Big E ʌ

Almost fifteen years after she commissioned the
Soft Big Easy (page 43), Patrizia Moroso asked Arad
to produce a plastic version of his original armchair.
The latest addition to the Big Easy family is made from
rotation-molded polyethylene, in red, white, black,
or blue. The chair's material is waterproof and resistant
to sunlight and changes in temperature, so it can be
used both indoors and outdoors.

The Big E. 2003
Rotation-molded polyethylene
36¹⁵⁄₁₆ × 51³⁄₈ × 33¼" (93.5 × 130.5 × 84.5 cm)
Manufactured by Moroso SpA, Italy

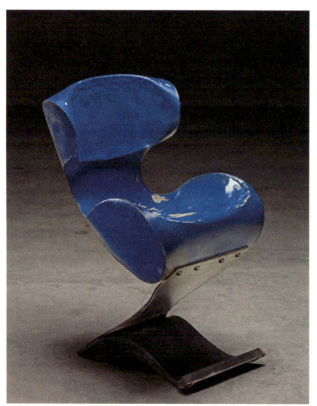

∧Spring Collection

Iconic design pieces are sometimes the result of the relationship between a designer and a manufacturer, like that of Arad and Patrizia Moroso, with the Soft Big Easy (page 43). The Spring Collection, introduced to the public in 1990, featured the Soft Big Easy along with eleven other pieces, some inspired by steel precedents—such as the Soft Little Heavy and the Soft Little Easy—and some entirely new shapes. Some of these were eventually abandoned at the prototype phase; the series currently in production features six pieces.

Spring Collection. Prototypes. 1990
Painted steel and tempered steel
Dimensions variable
Prototypes by Ron Arad for Moroso, Italy

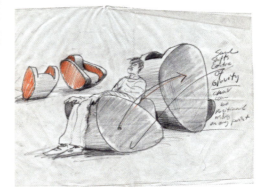

Rolling Volumes ^

Rolling Volumes are large rocking armchairs that were produced at Arad's Chalk Farm Road Studio (pages 134–36), where Arad moved his design and production activities in 1989. Two series of twenty chairs were made, one in mild steel and the other in mirror-polished stainless steel. The design began, in the prototype, with parallel sides, which in the final versions tapered toward the back of the chair. The chairs are heavily weighted at the back with lead ballast (originally sand), inverting the conventional operation of rocking: when not in use the chair tilts upward, and while in motion it provides an invisible force that plays against the sitter's weight.

Rolling Volume. 1991 [top left]
Mirror-polished stainless steel
30¾ × 35⁷⁄₁₆ × 37⅜" (78 × 90 × 95 cm)
Edition by One Off, London
Rolling Volume. 1992 [top right]
Polished stainless steel and red lacquer
31½ × 35⁷⁄₁₆ × 37⅜" (80 × 90 × 95 cm)
Edition by One Off, London

Rolling Volume. 1989 [center right]
Patinated mild steel and polished stainless steel
31½ × 33½ × 37⅜" (80 × 85 × 95 cm)
Edition by One Off, London
Sketches for Rolling Volume (1989). N.d. [bottom left & right]

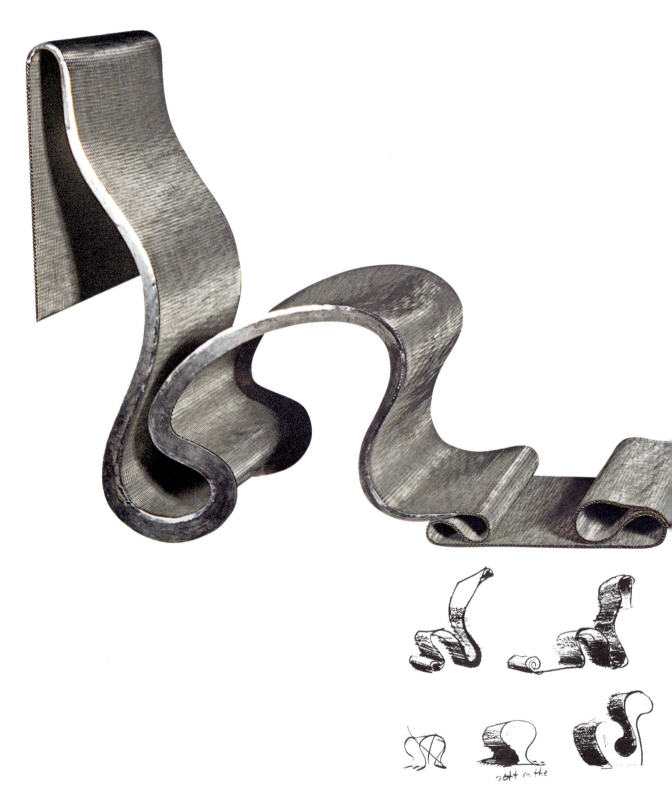

Narrow Papardelle. 1992
Woven stainless steel mesh and steel
40³/₁₆" × 6' 9⁵/₁₆" × 23⁵/₈" (102 × 206.5 × 60 cm)
Edition by One Off / Ron Arad Associates, London

Sketch for Papardelle (1992). N.d. [bottom]

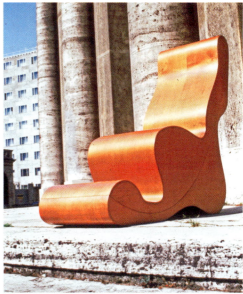

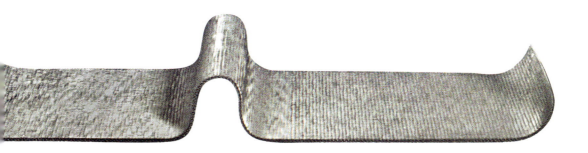

<Papardelle

A sinuous noodle of flexible woven steel, partly welded
to a stabilizing structure and left loose in the back
of the chair and in the front (where it can be rolled into
a footrest), Papardelle is one of Arad's iconic seats.
The steel textile, a rough material similar to that used
for conveyor belts, was an experiment here but became
a recurrent element in other early-1990s furniture
designs. A Suitable Case is Papardelle's cherrywood
storage box and a chair in itself; Looploop is a con-
densed version, using only the stable, "undercooked"
part of Papardelle.

Looploop. 1992 [top left]
Woven stainless steel mesh and steel
48⅝×16⅛×26" (123.5×41×66 cm)
Edition by One Off / Ron Arad Associates, London

A Suitable Case. 1994 [top right]
Cherrywood
Dimensions unknown
Edition by One Off / Ron Arad Associates, London

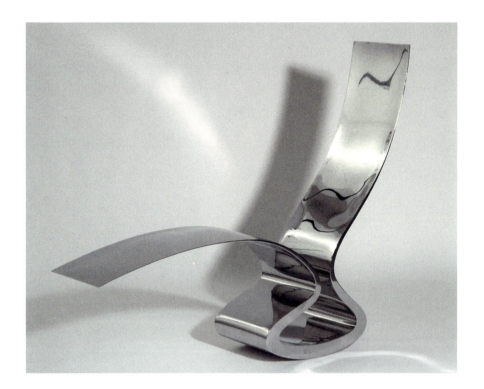

∧Before Summer
& After Spring>

After his first pieces made from sprung steel (pages
40–41) and his Spring Collection (page 50), Arad
designed After Spring, so named because the spring was
hidden yet still allowed for a resilient feel. Arad told art
critic Matthew Collings that it is a chair "in one line,
thickening in the center and tapering to the extremes.
The rocking base appears to be too small to support
the rocking movement, but is made stable by the heavy
internal weighting. The thin ends contain tempered-
steel springy 'bones' that give them strength and
flexibility." Before Summer is a similarly balanced chair,
with a higher back.

Before Summer. 1992 [top]
Mirror-polished stainless steel
51⁹⁄₁₆" × 6' 7⁷⁄₈" × 15" (131 × 208 × 38 cm)
Edition by One Off / Ron Arad Associates, London
Sketches for Before Summer (1992)
and After Spring (1992). N.d. [bottom]

After Spring. 1992
Patinated steel
43 5/16" × 6' 7 7/8" × 15" (110 × 208 × 38 cm)
Edition by One Off / Ron Arad Associates, London

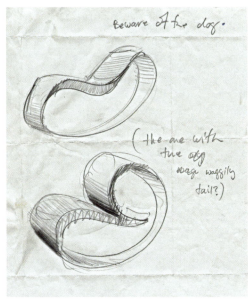

Beware of the Dog. 1990 [top]
Patinated steel and tempered sprung steel
28×22⁷⁄₁₆×70⁷⁄₈" (71×57×180 cm)
Edition by One Off/Ron Arad Associates, London
Sketches for Beware of the Dog (1990)
and Old Dog New Tricks (1990). N.d. [bottom right]

Old Dog New Tricks, Bucking Bronco, and Sit!
Prototypes. 1990 [bottom left]
Patinated steel and tempered sprung steel
Old Dog New Tricks: dimensions unknown;
Bucking Bronco: 44¹¹⁄₁₆"×12"×6' 2¹³⁄₁₆" (113.5×30.5×190 cm);
Sit!: 38⁹⁄₁₆×24³⁄₈×40³⁄₁₆" (98×62×102 cm)
Prototypes by One Off/Ron Arad Associates, London

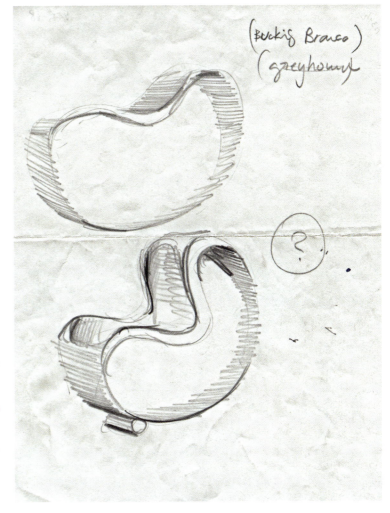

Vitra Design Museum Workshop

These chaises, surprisingly stable despite their narrow bases, provide a new experience: sitters neither rock nor simply lie still but bounce with the kind of trembling elasticity—and unique sound—that only tempered steel can provide. The chairs were made during a workshop Arad conducted at the Vitra Design Museum, in Weil am Rhein, Germany, in 1990. He had asked to be provided with tempered steel, the same material he had used for Vitra's edition of the Well Tempered Chair (pages 40–41), but it was available only in strips about twelve inches wide. Arad made a virtue out of necessity—and a new typology of chairs.

Sit! 1991 [top left]
Patinated steel and polished steel
34⅝×24¾×45¹¹/₁₆" (88×63×116 cm)
Edition by One Off, London, and The Gallery Mourmans, The Netherlands
Sit! Prototype. 1990 [bottom left]
Tempered and patinated steel
38⁹/₁₆×24⅜×40³/₁₆" (98×62×102 cm)
Prototype by Ron Arad/One Off, London

Bucking Bronco. Prototype. 1990 [top right]
Patinated steel and tempered sprung steel
44¹¹/₁₆"×12"×6' 2¹³/₁₆" (113.5×30.5×190 cm)
Prototype by Ron Arad/One Off, London
Sketches for Bucking Bronco (1990) **and Sit!** (1991). N.d. [bottom right]

This Mortal Coil. 1993
Tempered steel and riveted hinges
7' 5⁹⁄₁₆" × 7' 2¼" × 11¹³⁄₁₆" (227.5 × 219 × 30 cm)
Edition by One Off / Ron Arad Associates, London

This Mortal Coil

This Mortal Coil and One Way or Another are free-standing versions of Arad's successful Bookworm shelf (pages 60–63) and come from the same basic desire for a nonrectilinear system of bookshelves. This Mortal Coil is named for its snail-shell form as well as for its manner: it flexes and sways under the weight of books, creating an impression of suffering (although hardly at a Shakespearean level). Its form, made of blackened tempered steel, is held in shape with riveted hinges, allowing it to sway ever so gently without losing stability. One Way or Another, named by one of Arad's daughters for its side-to-side movement, also refuses to stay still. Both designs bring a sense of insecurity—even anxiety—to a familiar piece of furniture.

Sketches for This Mortal Coil (1993). N.d. [left & right]

One Way or Another. 1993 [following page, left]
Patinated steel and tempered sprung steel
7' 6⁹⁄₁₆" × 64¹⁵⁄₁₆" × 13" (230 × 165 × 33 cm)
Edition by One Off / Ron Arad Associates, London
Large Bookworm. 1993 [following page, right]
Tempered sprung steel and patinated steel
Bracket h. variable, 7⅞–11¹³⁄₁₆" (20–30 cm);
total l. 49' 2⁹⁄₁₆" (15 m); d. 13" (33 cm)
Edition by One Off / Ron Arad Associates, London

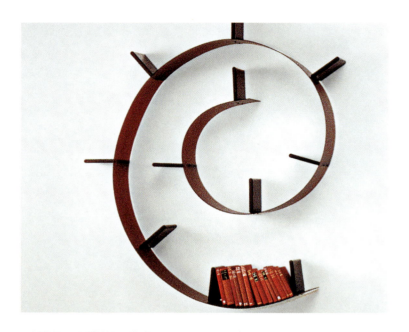

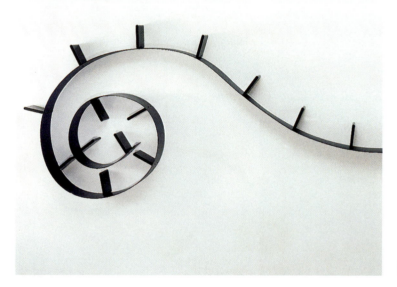

Bookworms

Although it began as another challenging, one-off piece, the Bookworm has become Arad's best-selling design. This quirky, tortuous shelf system proved so unexpectedly popular that it even became a best seller for its manufacturer, Kartell, which measures success in kilometers sold. Arad conceived the Bookworm in sprung steel, to make it both sculptural and functional, although in this form it was unreasonably demanding both to make and install, as well as quite expensive. Kartell took on the design and produced it in colorful, translucent, injection-molded PVC, thus making it accessible and attractive. The modular shelves could be tailored, like Arad's early Kee Klamp constructions, to suit individual and spatial requirements, through countless ways of linking its three-, five-, and eight-meter segments.

Bookworm 8005. 1993 [top]
Translucent, colored injection-molded PVC plastic
Bracket h. 7½" (19 cm), total l. 17' ¾" (520 cm), d. 7⅞" (20 cm)
Manufactured by Kartell, Italy

Bookworm 8008. 1993 [bottom]
Translucent, colored injection-molded PVC plastic
Bracket h. 7½" (19 cm), total l. 27' 8⅞" (820 cm), d. 7⅞" (20 cm)
Manufactured by Kartell, Italy

Sketch for Large Bookworm (1993). N.d. [right]

Sketch for Bookworm (1993). N.d.

^Lovely Rita

Arad loved to sing the Beatles song "Lovely Rita" when he was a teenager in Israel. Unfamiliar with the term "meter maid," he imagined the subject of the song to be a diminutive woman. Many years later he gave the name to this ribbonlike bookshelf, which is made in meter-long modules. Like the Bookworm, it can be used on its own or linked together with other modules to reach any length desired by the user.

Lovely Rita. 1996 [above]
Colored injection-molded PVC plastic
7⅞ × 39⅜ × 7⅞" (20 × 100 × 20 cm)
Manufactured by Kartell, Italy

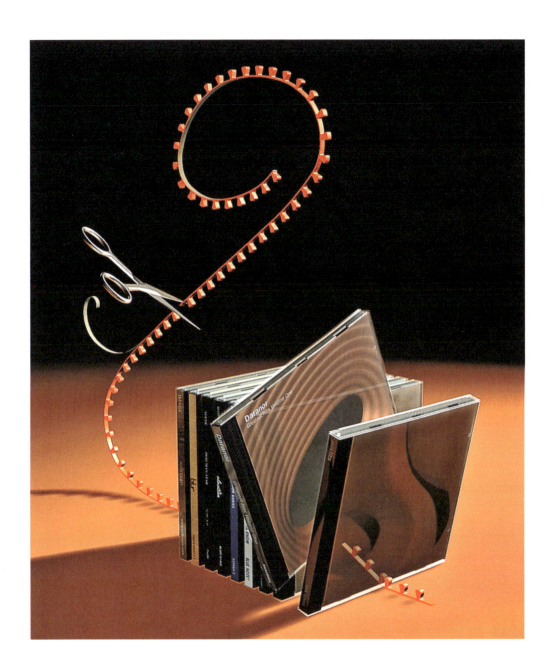

Rendering for Soundtrack (1998). N.d.

RON ARAD IN CONVERSATION WITH MARIE-LAURE JOUSSET

Marie-Laure Jousset:[1] Your first appearance at the Centre Pompidou was more than twenty years ago—*in Nouvelles Tendances,* in 1987.[2] So I would like to talk about you and the institution. What do you expect from institutions?

Ron Arad: An exhibition is your rapport with the public. And of course, nothing's perfect. If it were, I could do exactly what I wanted—but then it wouldn't be an institution. It would be another extension of what I do. So it's nice to have another filter. And it's very easy to drown everything you do with a rock of skepticism; to look at the things you do and think how pointless they are, how useless and pointless. Who needs another anything? You feel like a con artist. Conning *everyone.* Because all I want to do is have a good time and play and not do my homework and do things the way I want, and there aren't many ways to get feedback that reassures me that what I do is not completely meaningless.

And there are people whose opinion matters. Some of them are your old friends from art school, your reference points. Some of them are people you respect—industrialists, journalists, curators. So that's one thing. The other thing, unfortunately, is how well your pieces are doing on the market. It's not a nice discovery, but when you look at how a piece of yours does at auction, it gives you some indication of what meanings your things have next to other things. Then there are the institutions. People somehow have respect for institutions, even though they might be rebelling against them, mocking them, criticizing them.

MLJ: Which you keep doing.

RA: Sorry?

MLJ: *Which you keep doing.*

RA: Do I keep doing it? Do I? Ah. I'm sorry about that. But that's the way it is. Take the Royal Academy. You can't be more ridiculous than the Royal Academy, where, for the openings, they say you can wear your medals. All that pomp—not my planet! But it somehow cheers me to have a piece there. And it cheers me that it's not a painting. And it cheers me that it's not a piece of furniture. It's a bloody ping-pong table. It's *sports equipment.* And so sometimes you use the institution for your subversive activities.

When I had the show at the Victoria and Albert Museum, the front page of *The Daily Telegraph* screamed, "How did they allow this disgrace to happen?"[3] The reviewer was screaming and shouting about having plastic in the Victoria and Albert Museum. It made my day. It was proof that the exhibition was good and successful.

MLJ: Do you think that you are the best person to make curatorial decisions about your work? This is a big issue. Some American museums would say, "We should curate the show, instead of letting the artist do it himself." But I think that this is a perfect opportunity to give someone the chance to express his whole universe with almost no filter.

RA: I wish I didn't have to do any of the shit of curating and designing the show. I wish that it would all be done for me, and I could come a day before the opening and say, "Yes, great, lovely."

MLJ: I doubt that very much. You'd be too anxious.

RA: Ideally I'd like it to happen that way, but in reality I end up wanting to do everything myself. At MoMA I was talking to Paola Antonelli about this exhibition—it's not going to be exactly the same show as the one at the Pompidou because the space is different and some pieces will be different—so I said, "Look, why don't we do two different shows? We'll divide the space in half, and you do a show the way you think things should be shown, and I'll do another one." And for a few minutes I thought that was a great idea. Then reality kicked in.

MLJ: I think that if we're lucky enough to have designers living and active, we should take the opportunity to have them decide how their work should be presented: another work of art.

RA: It's part of what we do, designing spaces. But I'm very happy with the results of the various dialogues we had. We had to argue, to convince, to explain, to change.

MLJ: We have to explain to the public where the pieces come from, what they are. You're probably not as interested in that.

RA: I'm interested! For everything you do there are seven things you could have done and didn't. There's another story, another narrative that you want to tell.

MLJ: How do you feel about people trying to define you: "Is he a designer? An architect?" Are you afraid you will be judged as a bad artist, bad designer, and bad architect?

RA: I look forward to being judged as a good architect, good artist, and good designer. When you go into the studio, there are no borders between these functions—you don't need a passport to go from one to the other. I'm sorry if it makes life harder for people who like to put things in compartments.

As I said before, I like to have fun. My office works like a kindergarten—which is my way of not having to go to work, so you don't start the week groaning that it's Monday. And that's the basis of everything, this playground. I didn't plan to enter the design world. I was working in an architectural office, and I did a piece called The Rover Chair (pages 26–27). It's a readymade, but that's because it's what I was able to do at the time; not because I had a plan to save the world by recycling, and not because I wanted be a furniture designer. I just did it because I could.

MLJ: It was within your means and capabilities.

RA: It was doable. Then I was playing with concrete, working on the Concrete Stereo (pages 30–31), and I still didn't think of myself as a designer. If I had to compare it with something I would compare it with, I don't know, Meret Oppenheim's fur teacup before the iPod or Dieter Rams. And then, in 1987, some curator at the Pompidou invited me to be in this exhibition—big mistake!

MLJ: It wasn't!

RA: So all of a sudden I found myself in your museum, and I did something that had more to do with César and John Chamberlain than it did with Marcel Breuer and Charles Eames.[4]

I see a lot of cynical work. The market tells the art market that Design Art is doing well, but at the same time the art world doesn't accept design.

MLJ: There's a cultural difference: the art world always makes a lot of money but still doesn't want to talk about commercial things.

RA: I'm not interested in seeing a limited edition of Jasper Morrison's Crate.[5] I'm not happy that something like this is discussed in terms of Design Art. I see it as a sort of a marketing exercise. And on top of it, I'm blamed for Design Art: "You're complaining! You started it!"[6] Maybe I did. I didn't mean to. The real problem is that students of mine are going straight to it, but maybe there has been some development that is stronger than my understanding and my intentions. Which is good.

MLJ: I would say that you are a hero for younger generations of designers because you are a free man: you never go where someone wants you to go. But this is part of your personality.

RA: Maybe it's part of my—

MLJ: Your culture.

RA: —my limitation. You know? I'm not able to do things the way they're usually done. So I find other ways of doing things.

MLJ: You take new paths that no one else would dare to take.

RA: Yes, but it's not a question of courage. People find it very difficult to understand that I'm lazy and I'm not methodical. That's why I do so much.

MLJ: Lazy?

RA: Yes, in a way. I always rely on the people around me. I'm lucky that I have very good people around me, and talking to them is my best tool, even before drawing. I jump from one thing to the next. Like when The Rover Chair was a great success, I had to stop doing it because I didn't want to work by formula. I can easily destruct it and create new pet projects. And then it will be something else, and then it will be something else.

MLJ: You once said, "I have an imaginary museum in my mind, and I know and I enjoy work by Matisse without owning it." I think this is a very strong point.

RA: I owe a lot to museums. I don't come from the center of the world; I come from the periphery, but I did see exhibitions: a huge exhibition of van Gogh, a huge exhibition of Giacometti. And when people complain about how expensive my pieces are, I say, "Look there's a way to consume things without purchasing them." When I went to the Giacometti exhibition it never crossed my mind to think, "How much is this?" It's irrelevant.

I'm very happy with the name of the show, with *No Discipline.* Because it's exactly what I'm about. I don't need to define. You can use the Concrete Stereo as a piece of design. It's concrete; it uses the raw material of architecture. It uses the devices of art and it plays music, so it's art and design in one.

MLJ: So "no discipline" is your structure?

RA: Or my lack of structure. I'm not going to make a manifesto out of it, but this is what I do.

MLJ: In French we wouldn't say "no discipline." We would say *indiscipline.*

RA: What!

MLJ: *Indiscipline.* Here "in" means "without."

RA: I told some French people the title, and they sort of accepted it.

MLJ: No, we cannot.

RA: *Indiscipline.*

MLJ: *Indiscipline.* At first we wrote—

RA: —*hors discipline.* But "no discipline" is like *pas de discipline.*

MLJ: Is making enough money a problem now?

RA: We don't make much money. We feed the operation; it finances itself. I wish more money came in, so we wouldn't have to think twice about projects. We could do them without convincing anyone else or campaigning to raise money.

MLJ: Money gives you independence?

RA: Money makes it possible to make the things that I'm doing.

MLJ: But twenty years ago you had no money, and you still made things.

RA: Well, I made different things. And the work was always financed by the work. Yes, it's more comfortable now, but let's not get neurotic about it. For some people success, financial and otherwise, makes them do *worse* work. And some people enjoy success, and the work benefits from it.

MLJ: Do you think that your work, which is much more spectacular today than it was twenty years ago, is meeting those expectations? Do you still enjoy the balance between working with a manufacturing company and working independently?

RA: Look, at the same time that I do these very expensive pieces in small quantities, I am also very excited about the PizzaKobra (pages 182–83), which is industrial and, hopefully, for everyone. I would design for Ikea if the project was right and if it made sense. What I don't want to do is *not* design for Ikea so it's easier for some snotty, bullshitting art reviewers to look at the work that they should be looking at, and I don't want to do the opposite —I don't want to not do art pieces to keep Ikea interested. You don't have to align yourself with one side or the other.

MLJ: It was key for me to be able to show those different attitudes. Why did you decide to work with Kartell?

RA: Because design isn't about finishes, it's about materials. And Kartell is about plastic, which is a material that has its own finishes. I like the way plastic ages, and I like color. And I don't like cluttering things or covering things — not with paint and not with panels. If you look at most of my furniture, it's very rarely painted.

MLJ: Do you use color in your work?

RA: I use a lot of colors. I like the color of metal, I like the color of brass, I like the color of concrete, I like the color of wood. I love colors. I just don't like paint at the moment.

MLJ: You still don't like paint.

RA: I do like paint. There are no rules. But I like to let the material speak rather than use other materials to cover it. It's very simple. I don't like chrome. I like stainless steel, but chrome is a cover, a layer. But if I needed to use chrome for some reason, I wouldn't say, "Rule number thirty-one says no chrome." I'd use chrome.

MLJ: Are you ready for the exhibition's critics?

RA: I'm sure there will be critics. Only Nelson Mandela escapes criticism.

MLJ: Do you care about the opinion of the public?

RA: I want people to enjoy the exhibition and have a good time. I meet a lot of people, young Israeli people — maybe not so young now — who tell me, "I became a designer when I saw your show at the Tel Aviv Museum of Art."[7] Great! Lovely...

[1] This conversation took place in June 2008, in London.

[2] *Nouvelles Tendances: Les Avant-gardes de la fin du XXe siècle,* April 14–September 8, 1987, Centre Pompidou, Musée national d'art moderne–Centre de création industrielle, Paris. An exhibition catalogue of the same name was published by Éditions du Centre Georges Pompidou in 1986.

[3] The exhibition was the solo show *Ron Arad: Before and After Now,* June 13–October 1, 2000, at the Victoria and Albert Museum, London. A brochure was published to accompany the exhibition.

[4] For *Nouvelles Tendances,* Arad concocted a machine that crushed chairs, reducing them to bricks that could be used to build something new.

[5] Morrison, commissioned to design a bedside table, declared that he could not improve upon an old-fashioned wooden crate and proceeded to redesign one. The Crates, produced in 2007 by the United Kingdom–based company Established & Sons, are exactly what they claim to be: pinewood boxes that could accommodate oranges or wine. The painstaking attention paid to their making—they are equipped with colored fabric hinges and can be assembled to form storage units, beds, and other furnishings—as well as their price, have made them highly controversial. Established & Sons produces some of its catalogue pieces in limited series but not the Crates, which are part of its high-end serial production.

[6] Design Art denotes unique objects that can be construed as design—either because they have a designated function or because they are made by bona fide designers—and sold by art galleries or auction houses at prices well beyond those of their serially produced counterparts. Although such objects have for many years existed under the rubrics of craft and decorative art, their prices in the past seven or eight years have begun a heated discussion on the corrupting influence of the market on design.

[7] *Ron Arad: Recent Works,* 1990, Tel Aviv Museum of Art.

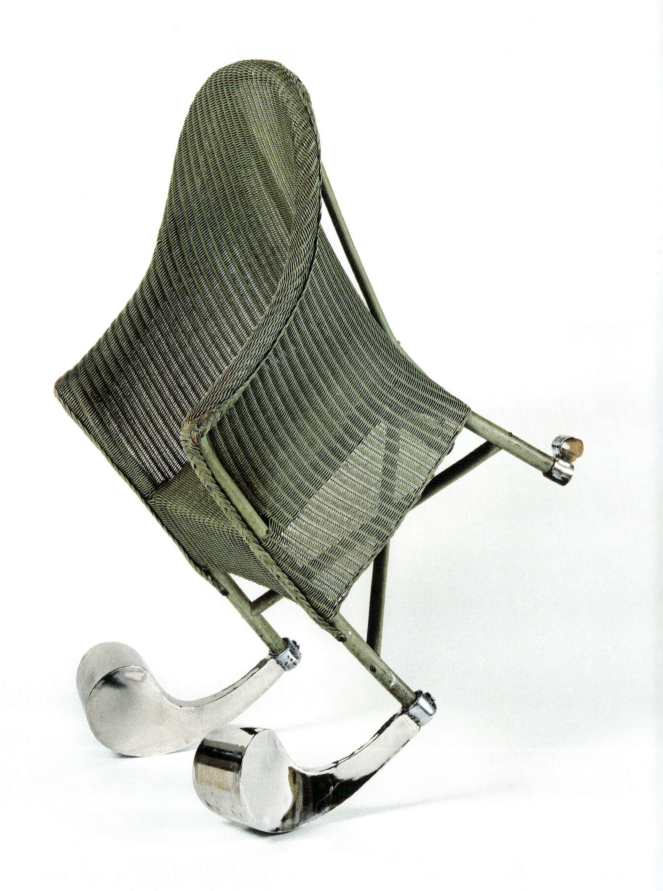

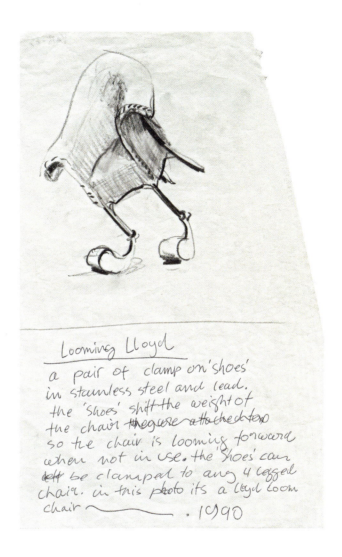

Looming Lloyd

a pair of clamp on 'shoes'
in stainless steel and lead.
the 'shoes' shift the weight of
the chair ~~the gere attached to~~
so the chair is looming forward
when not in use. the 'shoes' can
~~off~~ be clamped to any 4 legged
chair. in this ~~photo~~ its a lloyd loom
chair ——————. 1990

Looming Lloyd

This unstable seat is a hybrid readymade: a pair of
clamp-on weighted clogs that can be attached to any
four-legged chair to breathe new life into it—trans-
forming it into a tilting, tumbling, rocking wonder.

Looming Lloyd. 1989 [opposite]
Lloyd Loom chair, stainless steel, and patinated steel
36¼ × 41⁵⁄₁₆ × 25⁵⁄₁₆" (92 × 105 × 65 cm)
Edition by One Off / Ron Arad Associates, London
Sketch for Looming Lloyd (1989). N.d. [above]

chaise very longue
(wild crow)

<Wild Crow

Deyan Sudjic's 2001 book about Arad is called *Restless Furniture,* and that title is perhaps nowhere more resonant than in Wild Crow, the first and most distinctive among Arad's unstable seats. Wild Crow seems quite menacing, perched on its heavy and unstable base with its beak thrust towards the sky, until you dare to sit on it—at which point your courage is rewarded by a soothing, rocking chaise longue.

Spanish Made>

Spanish Made, so named because it was made during a workshop in Spain, is inscribed with the indigenous proverb "The dog barks, but the caravan moves on."

Wild Crow. 1988 [left]
Stainless steel and patinated steel
69 ⅝ × 19 ⅝ × 17 ⁵⁄₁₆" (177 × 50 × 44 cm)
Edition by One Off, London
Sketch for Wild Crow (1988). N.d. [right]

Spanish Made. 1990
Stainless steel
37¾ × 24¾ × 31½" (96 × 63 × 80 cm)
Edition by One Off / Ron Arad Associates, London

A.Y.O.R

∧At Your Own Risk (A.Y.O.R.)

A.Y.O.R. (At Your Own Risk) tips forward so danger-ously, because of its ballast, that it barely resembles a chair. It rather looks like an apostrophe, albeit a threatening and cartoonish one. Arad dares you to try to sit—and the comfort and balance are well worth the feeling of mastery over this unbalanced thing (see also page 14, FIG 5 | FIG 6).

Box in Four Movements>

This chair is as straightforward as its name: one box, four sections, three hinges, four movements. The hinges are set on a torsion bar that provides a springy, surprisingly bouncy action; it can be adjusted with an electric screwdriver that comes with the chair, and sits on casters that lock automatically when the chair is in use. Here Arad once again plays with the contrast between material and comfort—although the feeling of comfort is somewhat limited.

At Your Own Risk (A.Y.O.R.). 1991 [top left]
Mirror-polished stainless steel with iron counterbalance
37 3/8 × 21 5/8 × 19 5/8" (95 × 55 × 50 cm)
Edition by One Off, London, 1991–99, and The Gallery Mourmans,
The Netherlands, 2000–2007
Sketch for At Your Own Risk (A.Y.O.R.) (1991). N.d. [top right]

At Your Own Risk (A.Y.O.R.). 1991 [bottom]
Polished steel with lead ballast
39 5/8 × 18 1/2 × 19 5/8" (100.5 × 47 × 50 cm)
Edition by One Off, London, 1991–99, and The Gallery Mourmans,
The Netherlands, 2000–2007

Sketch for Box in Four Movements (1994). N.d. [top]
Box in Four Movements. 1994
Stainless steel with torsion bars [bottom left] or
polished and patinated bronze with torsion bars [bottom right]
Extended: 32×15¾×15¾" (81.5×40×40 cm);
closed: 16¾×15¾×15¾" (42.5×40×40 cm)
Edition by Ron Arad Associates, London

and the Rabbit speaks!   *R Arad 94*

∧Schizzo

When Rolf Fehlbaum, chairman of Vitra, asked Arad to design a space-saving chair, Arad responded with Schizzo (Italian for "sketch"), which is inspired by the concept of a stacking chair but differs in its outcome: a double chair that can be pulled apart into two separate units, and so can only be "stacked" two at a time—horizontally, into each other. Schizzo is packed in an aluminum case (And the Rabbit Speaks) that can itself serve as a chair. This piece, one of Arad's few designs in wood, is made of bent plywood laminated in wide bands and then sliced.

And the Rabbit Speaks. 1994 [top left]
Anodized aluminum with Alcantara lining
Dimensions unknown
Edition by Ron Arad Associates, London
Sketches for Schizzo (1989) **and**
And the Rabbit Speaks (1994). N.d. [bottom]

Schizzo. 1989 [right]
Plywood
35¼ × 22 × 14⅛" (89.5 × 56 × 36 cm)
Manufactured by Vitra GmbH, Germany

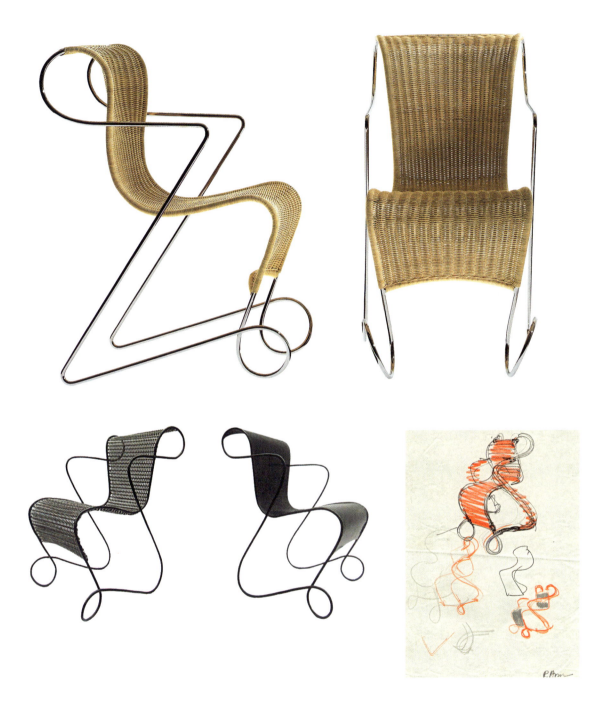

Zigo. 1992 [top]
Stainless steel and rattan
34⅝×20⅞×24" (88×53×61 cm)
Manufactured by Driade SpA, Italy

Zigo and Zago. Models. 1992 [bottom left]
Patinated steel and steel mesh
Dimensions unknown
Models by Ron Arad Associates, London
Sketches for Zigo (1992) **and Zago** (1992). N.d. [bottom right]

Tel Aviv Performing
Arts Center

In 1988 Ron Arad Associates won the competition that
led to the design of the foyer of the Tel Aviv Performing
Arts Center, designed by architect Yacov Rechter.
Six years later it was completed and became Arad's
most famous architectural realization. It is a dramatic
and joyous space in which different elements — the
bookshop, the staircase, the café — come together
to conjure a feeling of spectacle and wonderment.

Tel Aviv Performing Arts Center. 1988–94

∧Empty Chair

The Empty Chair, designed for the Tel Aviv Performing Arts Center (pages 84–85), later became part of a plywood-and-steel series, manufactured by the Italian company Driade, which also includes a table and a tea trolley.

Empty Chair. Prototype. 1994 [top left]
Lacquered plywood with paint and handwritten instructions
37 × 20⅞ × 22¹³⁄₁₆" (94 × 53 × 58 cm)
Prototype by Ron Arad and Driade SpA, Italy
Sketch for Empty Chair (1994). N.d. [bottom]

Empty Chair. 1994 [right]
Ash plywood and stainless steel
36⅝ × 20½ × 23" (93 × 52 × 58.2 cm)
Manufactured by Driade SpA, Italy

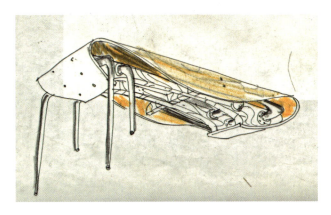

Fly Ply. 1994 [top]
Ash plywood and cast aluminum
29½" × 6' 10⅝" × 37" (75 × 210 × 94 cm)
Manufactured by Driade SpA, Italy
Sketch for Fly Ply (1994). N.d. [bottom]

Tom Vac

Many of Arad's furniture designs could stand on their own as sculptures despite their functional beginnings, but the Tom Vac, named for photographer and friend Tom Vack, began as an actual sculpture. In 1997 *Domus* magazine commissioned Arad to design an installation for the Milan Furniture Fair, and he decided that this would take the form of one hundred chairs stacked in the center of a busy intersection in the center of the city. Instead of using existing chairs, he put the project budget toward a machine that could vacuum-form an aluminum chair in twenty minutes—an efficient process for the sculpture, which Arad had to complete in four months, with an additional limited edition of the new chairs. The industrially produced version, developed by Vitra, is made of injection-molded plastic. It is a versatile piece, characterized by wide ribs and concentric waves and a back aperture in the seat—features later echoed in the Ripple Chair (pages 108–9)—that has become one of Arad's most popular mass-produced designs.

Domus Totem. 1997 [opposite]
Installation in Milan, Salone del Mobile, 1997
Tom Vac. 1999 [overlay, opposite]
Molded polypropylene and tubular steel
30 × 26⅜ × 22⅞" (76 × 67 × 58 cm)
Manufactured by Vitra GmbH, Germany

Sketch for Tom Vac (1997). N.d. [top]
Tom Rock. 1999 [center]
Molded polypropylene, tubular steel, and plywood
24½ × 23 × 30" (62.3 × 58.4 × 76 cm)
Manufactured by Vitra GmbH, Germany
Tom Vac. 1997 [right]
Vacuum-formed polished aluminum sheet and tubular steel
29½ × 25¼ × 25⅝" (75 × 64 × 60 cm)
Edition by Ron Arad Studio, Italy

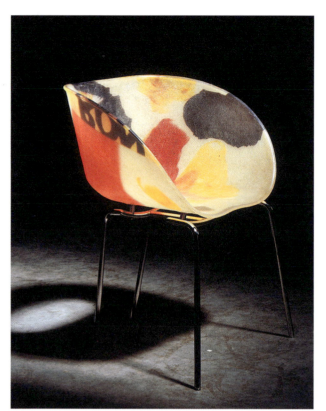

Pic Chairs

Pic Chairs (or "pictures") are decorated versions of the
Tom Vac (pages 88–89), produced in an edition of
twenty unique pieces. Arad produced these handmade
fiberglass chairs as studies while he was waiting for
production of the Tom Vac to begin. He experimented
with applying pigments, polyester, newspaper, tissue,
and luminous wire directly to the mold before the fiberglass was inserted; the results look ahead to the 1999
New Orleans chairs (page 48).

Pic Chairs. 1997
Fiberglass, polyester, and pigment
32¼ × 28 × 23¼" (82 × 71 × 59 cm)
Edition by Ron Arad for The Gallery Mourmans, The Netherlands

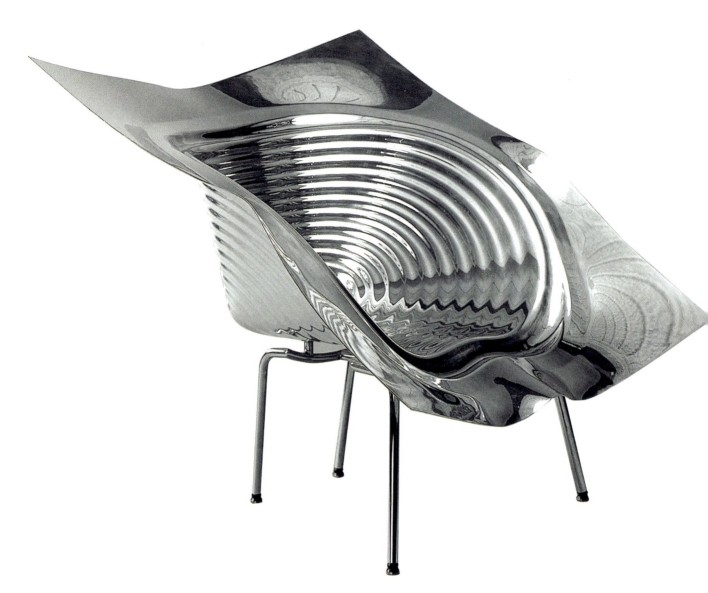

∧Uncut

Thick Vac>
Tom Block>

Uncut is a Tom Vac chair (pages 88–89) with the extra aluminum around the seat left untrimmed, and, like the original, it is vacuum-formed from aluminum, either mirror polished or anodized, and mounted on a low, sculptural, stainless steel base. Almost a decade later Arad produced two more iterations of this popular form, Thick Vac and Tom Block—chunky, polished aluminum chairs, each developed from two untrimmed Tom Vacs. These premiered at Arad's 2006 exhibition at de Pury & Luxembourg, his first show in Switzerland. They contrast sharply with the lightness and versatility of their mass-produced forebears.

Uncut. 1997
Vacuum-formed aluminum sheet and polished stainless steel
32⅝×38⅝×35" (83×98×89 cm)
Edition by Ron Arad Studio, Italy

Thick Vac. 2006 [top]
Polished aluminum
38⅝ × 43⁵⁄₁₆ × 32¼" (98 × 110 × 82 cm)
Edition by The Gallery Mourmans, The Netherlands

Tom Block. 2006 [bottom]
Polished aluminum
39 × 37 × 33⅞" (99 × 94 × 86 cm)
Edition by The Gallery Mourmans, The Netherlands

FPE

FPE (Fantastic, Plastic, Elastic) is an inexpensive stacking chair made from lightweight plastic and aluminum. The design, originally conceived in plywood (as the Cross Your T's Chair), was part of a commission from Mercedes-Benz for a transportable exhibition stand that would be taken to motor shows in Europe. The chair was not suited to small-scale production, and was therefore tweaked and perfected for mass manufacture. Its final form is exceptional in the simplicity of its construction: a plastic seat is inserted into channels in double-barreled extruded aluminum profiles, which, when the chair frame is bent, hold the plastic in place. With no need for glue, screws, or bolts, this method allows the simplest combination of frame and plane to create a sinuous, practical, resilient form—proving Arad's ability to embrace industrial production and make the best of its possibilities. The FPE can be stacked in groups of eight, comes in three colors (opaline, blue, and red, although it was originally available in yellow), and can be used both indoors and out.

FPE (Fantastic, Plastic, Elastic). 1997 [left & right]
Extruded aluminum profiles and injection-molded polypropylene
plastic sheet
31¼×17×22" (79.4×43.2×55.9 cm)
Manufactured by Kartell, Italy
Sketch for FPE (Fantastic, Plastic, Elastic) (1997). N.d. [opposite]

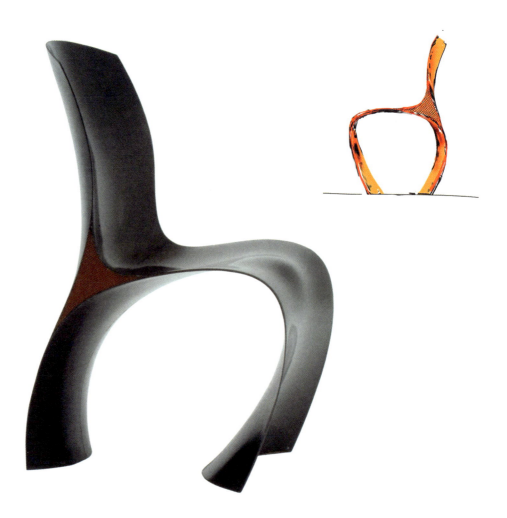

Paperwork Collection

The Paperwork Collection, produced by The Gallery Mourmans and made up of two desks (All Light Long and Moby's Trip) plus three chairs (3 Skin Joint, Oh-Void 1, and Oh-Void 2 [pages 110–11]), was first introduced at the 2002 Milan Furniture Fair, in an exhibition at the Galleria Gió Marconi. The pieces are made out of cured carbon fiber with an internal core of Nomex honeycomb, and thus are surprisingly light. Some have a high-tech gloss; others have a worn-out, familiar feel, as if they had been around for generations. The 3 Skin Joint was picked up by Moroso, to be mass-produced as the 3 Skin Chair, in multilayered, lacquered wood.

3 Skin Chair. 2003 [left]
Plywood
31½ × 19¼ × 26¾" (85 × 49 × 68 cm)
Manufactured by Moroso SpA, Italy

3 Skin Joint. 2002 [center]
Carbon fiber and Nomex
36¼ × 19⅝ × 24⅜" (92 × 50 × 62 cm)
Edition by The Gallery Mourmans, The Netherlands
Sketch for 3 Skin Joint (2002). N.d. [right]

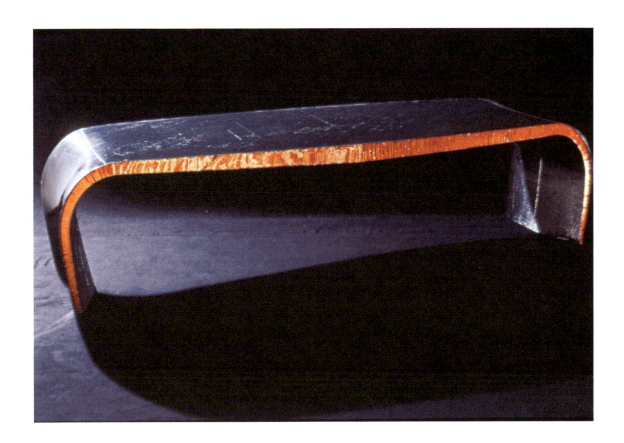

All Light Long. 2002 [top]
Carbon fiber and Nomex
31½" × 9' 6³⁄₁₆" × 39⅜" (80 × 290 × 100 cm)
Edition by The Gallery Mourmans, The Netherlands

Moby's Trip. 2002 [bottom]
Carbon fiber and Nomex
36¼" × 6' 8⁵⁄₁₆" × 30" (92 × 204 × 76 cm)
Edition by The Gallery Mourmans, The Netherlands

Cappellone

Arad has always liked hats, and even claims to choose his cars based on whether they have a sunroof or roof high enough to accommodate them. He designed Cappellone (Italian for "big hat") for himself, a unisex wool-felt hat in a unique form that echoes and blends familiar shapes: bowler, baseball cap, cloche, beret, panama hat, and riding helmet. Cappellone, which has become something of a trademark look for the designer, was manufactured by Alessi, in collaboration with the renowned hatmaker Borsalino. Arad had already worked with Alessi on his Soundtrack CD rack (page 65) and BabyBoop Bowls and Vase (page 120) when managing director Alberto Alessi approached him about this, which became the company's first clothing product. It was produced in a limited edition of one thousand and was sold at the opening of the Alessi showroom in London, in 2000. Cappellone has been reeditioned by The Museum of Modern Art, New York.

Cappellone. 2000
Wool felt
11¹³/₁₆ × 11¹³/₁₆ × 7 ⅞" (30 × 30 × 20 cm)
Manufactured by Alessi SpA, Italy

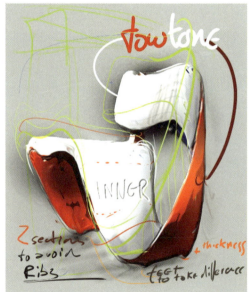

Renderings for Swan Chair (2001–4). N.d. [top & bottom left]
Sketch for Swan Chair (2001–4). N.d. [bottom right]

<Swan Chair

Arad has noted that design used to come from the pencil, but now it comes from the screen. For the Swan Chair he meticulously tweaked the form and structure of computer-generated images until he was satisfied with the result, which is made from a single twisted band. (By the time the alterations were complete, the chair no longer resembled the swan of the original design, but the name remained.) Although this process seems unrelated to the methods he used for his earlier furniture, especially the metal studio pieces, Arad has compared these gradual changes to the way he refined the design of the Tinker Chair (pages 38–39) with a rubber hammer. Originally conceived in plastic, the Swan Chair was executed in aluminum with a wavy surface similar to the early studio version of the Tom Vac (pages 88–89). It is a stacking chair that also connects sideways (the legs fit into each other to create continuous rows).

Nina Rota & None Rota^

Each chair and each armchair is obtained from a single rotation-molded form that is then cut in half, a very efficient manufacturing process. Their names pay tribute to the great Nino Rota, Federico Fellini's favorite composer, as well as playing on the name of the process that creates them.

Rendering for Nina Rota and None Rota (2002). N.d. [top]
Sketch for Nina Rota and None Rota (2002). N.d. [bottom]

MT

Arad's work often begins as a studio piece that is later adapted for industrial production, but in some cases the direction is reversed, as was the case with the MT (or "empty") series. Intrigued by the untapped potential of rotation-molding, one of the humblest methods of manufacturing plastic products, Arad came up with beautiful, complex concave/convex forms, highlighted by contrasting colors, for an armchair, rocker, and couch. The MT collection is manufactured by Driade, but Arad subsequently translated the rocking piece into versions made of polished stainless steel or bronze, using an exquisite technique involving the patient application, by hand, of metal rods onto a basic structure.

MT Rocker Chair, 2006
Polished bronze rods
29 × 33½ × 40" (73.7 × 85.1 × 101.6 cm)
Edition by Ron Arad Associates, London

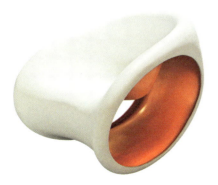

MT Rocker Chair. 2005 [top]
Polished stainless steel rods
29×33½×40" (73.7×85.1×101.6 cm)
Edition by Ron Arad Associates, London

MT3. 2005 [bottom left]
Rotation-molded polyethylene
30¹¹⁄₁₆×31½×40¹⁵⁄₁₆" (78×80×104 cm)
Manufactured by Driade SpA, Italy

MT1. 2005 [bottom right]
Rotation-molded polyethylene
32⅝×29×29⅛" (83×73.5×74 cm)
Manufactured by Driade SpA, Italy

∧Victoria and Albert

Victoria and Albert is named for the famous decorative
arts and design museum in South Kensington, London,
the location of Arad's 2000 solo exhibition, *Before and
After Now*. It is a bright and easy variation of Arad's
recurring reclining figure-eight form, in a steel support
covered with polyurethane foam, in varying densities,
and reinforced polyester resin. The sofa is the centerpiece of the Victoria and Albert Collection, designed
for Moroso, which includes coffee tables of rotation-
molded polyethylene, a steel-and-foam armchair much
like the sofa, and (later) the Little Albert.

Victoria and Albert, 2002
Reinforced polyester, steel, and polyurethane foam
56" × 9' 9" × 48⅞" (142 × 297 × 123 cm)
Manufactured by Moroso SpA, Italy

Little Albert ∧

Little Albert was born when Patrizia Moroso asked Arad to add a small armchair to his Victoria and Albert Collection. Like The Big E (page 49), these chairs are made from rotation-molded polyethylene; Arad credits fellow British designer Tom Dixon (who also came to design by way of another career, as an artist, and who also set up his studio in London in the early 1980s) with being the first to use this method, a very slow and primitive one, but the most inexpensive way to create furniture from plastic. The chair's tapered shape can be made with a simple, two-part mold, and the resulting forms are available in many colors, with either a glossy or matte finish, and are recyclable as well. The chairs made their debut in 2005, at the Cologne Furniture Fair.

Little Albert. 2002
Rotation-molded polyethylene
29½ × 29⅛ × 29½" (75 × 74 × 75 cm)
Manufactured by Moroso SpA, Italy

∧Evergreen!

Evergreen! — in Arad's records titled with an exclamation point, and in the Japanese press appended with a question mark — is a public sculpture commissioned by the administration of Roppongi Hills, the massive new development in central Tokyo where Arad also designed a store for Yohji Yamamoto (pages 173–77). On the occasion of the development's opening, in 2003, the Roppongi Hills administration asked eleven designers from all over the world to provide solutions for furniture to be placed along the street. Arad's bench, an extended figure-eight form made of bronze pipe that is meant to be colonized by ivy and become part of the landscape, is a favorite with the public.

Evergreen! 2003
Bronze and ivy
8' 10¹¹/₁₆" × 19' 9¹³/₁₆" × 58¼" (271×604×148 cm)
Installation in Roppongi Hills, Tokyo

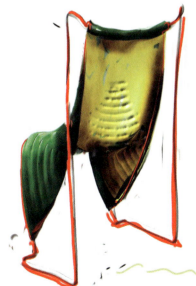

Wavy ∧

Using materials in a manner both striking and playful, Arad made this stackable chair with a steel structure and a ribbed, thermoformed shell that looks like a piece of cloth thrown over it. Moroso, the manufacturer, is currently working on a two-toned version.

Wavy. 2007 [top]
Thermoformed colored ABS plastic and stainless steel
38⅝×25⅜×26" (98×64×66 cm)
Manufactured by Moroso SpA, Italy
Sketch for Wavy (2007). N.d. [bottom]

Ripple Chair

This concave figure-eight seat (resembling a butterfly, mask, pretzel, or Zen tracing in the sand) is made of injection-molded thermoplastic, a malleable material ideally suited to highlighting Ripple's soft waves in relief. Manufactured and distributed by Moroso, this chair is stackable and suitable for both indoor and outdoor use. In 2006 Arad collaborated with fashion designer Issey Miyake to design an "outfit" for Ripple that could also be worn by its owner—a marriage of fashion and design. The project was part of a concept developed by Miyake and textile engineer Dai Fujiwara, called A Piece of Cloth (A-POC), in which a continuous length of fabric (wool, cotton, or down) is produced by a computer and extruded by a machine. Ripple's version is meant to be worn as a jacket, with the seat-aperture openings also functioning as armholes.

Ripple Chair. 2006 [top]
Injection-molded polypropylene shell and stainless steel base
31½ × 26¾ × 23¼" (80 × 68 × 59 cm)
Manufactured by Moroso SpA, Italy
Sketch for Ripple Chair (2005–6). N.d. [bottom]

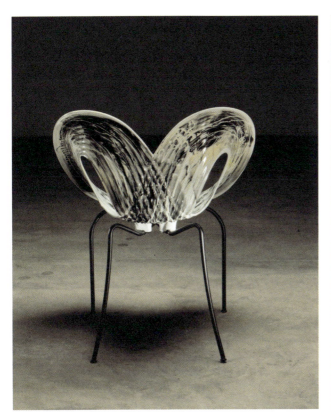

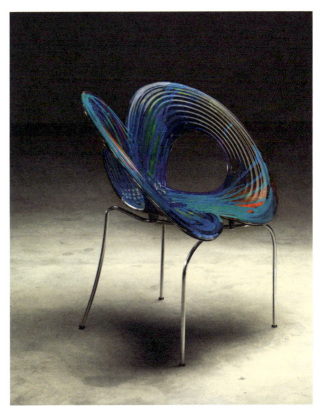

Ron Arad with Issey Miyake and Dai Fujiwara of Miyake Design Studio
Ripple Chair Dressed with A-POC (A Piece of Cloth). 2006 [bottom left]
Injection-molded polypropylene shell, varnished steel base, and A-POC
(woven polyester and cotton) textile
A-POC: 26⅜ × 30¹¹/₁₆" (67 × 78 cm)
Manufactured by Moroso SpA, Italy, and Miyake Design Studio, Japan

Ripple Chair. Prototypes. 2005 [top left & right, bottom right]
Fiberglass, polyester, and gelcoat shell on steel base
31½ × 26¾ × 23¼" (80 × 68 × 59 cm)
Prototypes by Moroso SpA, Italy, hand-painted by Ron Arad

The Voids

The Voids family, together with the Volumes (pages 40–49) are Arad's most populous series. The Voids are formed by two ellipses joined into a rocking body that is also a comfortable chaise longue. From this basic DNA, Arad created different chairs by varying his materials, proportions, colors, weights, voids, and special effects. The first variant, made in 2003 as part of the Paperwork Collection (pages 96–97), was an experiment with carbon fiber, a very light material, followed by versions in Corian and superplastic aluminum, and spectacular versions made in acrylic and silicone. All of the Voids were produced in limited editions, except for Voido, which is manufactured by the Italian company Magis.

The Corian Oh-Voids (top left and right) were carved from blocks made of slices of red or black Corian bonded together with an adhesive in a contrasting color. The carving revealed veins and rings like an old tree trunk's. The acrylic Oh-Voids (on the facing page) are made in a similar manner to the Corian Oh-Void 2, but here color layers alternate with transparent layers, giving the colors, which cast shadows and reflect light, a physicality of their own.

Oh-Void 1. 2004 [top left]
Corian
45⅝" × 6' 5⁹⁄₁₆" × 18⅛" (116 × 197 × 46 cm)
Edition by The Gallery Mourmans, The Netherlands
Sketch for Oh-Void 1 (2004). N.d. [center left]
Oh-Void 1. 2002 [bottom]
Composite of aramid fibers and Nomex
45⅝" × 6' 5⁹⁄₁₆" × 18⅛" (116 × 197 × 46 cm)
Edition by The Gallery Mourmans, The Netherlands

Oh-Void 2. 2004 [top right]
Corian
23⅝ × 44⅞ × 27³⁄₁₆" (60 × 114 × 69 cm)
Edition by The Gallery Mourmans, The Netherlands
Sketch for Oh-Void 2 (2004). N.d. [center right]

Oh-Void 2. 2006 [top]
Acrylic
30¼×43×23⅝" (76.8×109.2×60 cm)
Edition by The Gallery Mourmans, The Netherlands

Oh-Void 1. 2006 [bottom left]
Acrylic
45¾"×6' 6½"×18½" (116.2×199.4×47 cm)
Edition by The Gallery Mourmans, The Netherlands

Oh-Void 2. 2008 [bottom right]
Acrylic
25¹³⁄₁₆×45¼×23⅝" (65.5×115×60 cm)
Edition by The Gallery Mourmans, The Netherlands

<∧There Is No Solution

"There is no solution, because there is no problem." Marcel Duchamp's words are inscribed in the original French and in English on the twisted steel spine spiraling through this transparent Oh-Void. In an interview with *Interiors* magazine, Arad declared that he sometimes feels that he is solving problems that do not exist, adding objects to a world already full of design; after a pause that seems uncanny for a designer who has never refrained from pushing and experimenting, Arad exorcized his doubt by casting it in silicone.

There Is No Solution. 2006 [previous page]
Silicone and steel
27 ⁹/₁₆ × 47 ¼ × 25 ⅝" (70 × 120 × 65 cm)
Edition by The Gallery Mourmans, The Netherlands
Sketch for There Is No Solution (2006). N.d. [above]

No-Void. 2006 [above]
Mirror-polished aluminum and aluminum mesh
52⁵/₁₆" × 7' 1" × 7⅞" (133 × 216 × 20 cm)
Edition by The Gallery Mourmans, The Netherlands

Blo-Void 1. 2006 [top]
Polished lacquered aluminum
40"×6' 8"×17" (101.6×203.2×43.2 cm)
Edition by The Gallery Mourmans, The Netherlands

Blo-Void 1. 2005 [bottom]
Polished aluminum
43"×6' 7⅛"×17" (109×201×43 cm)
Edition by The Gallery Mourmans, The Netherlands

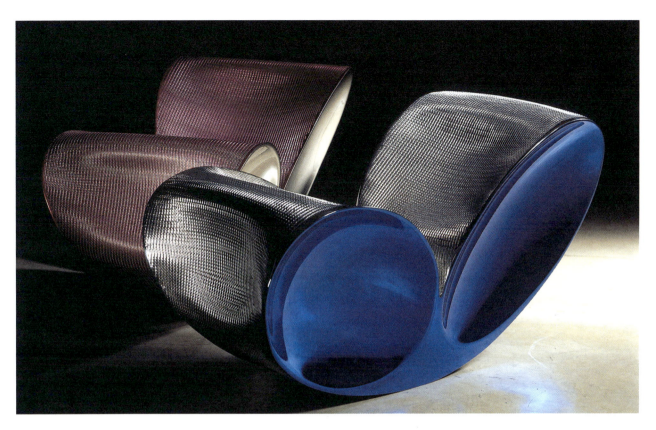

Blo-Void 2. 2006 [top]
Lacquered anodized aluminum
28 7/16 × 45 5/8 × 22" (72 × 116 × 56 cm)
Edition by The Gallery Mourmans, The Netherlands
Sketch for Blo-Void 2 (2006). N.d. [bottom]

Voido. 2006
Polyethylene
30¾ × 44⅞ × 22⅞" (78 × 114 × 58 cm)
Manufactured by Magis SpA, Italy

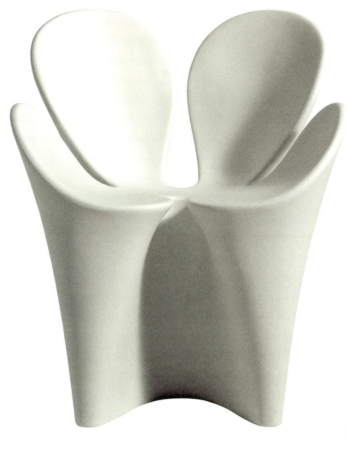

Clover. 2007
Polyethylene
29¾ × 26 × 21¼" (75.5 × 66 × 54 cm)
Manufactured by Driade SpA, Italy

Blown Out Of Proportion (B.O.O.P.) Table. 1998 [top left]
Superplastic aluminum
13 × 53⅛ × 37" (33 × 135 × 94 cm)
Edition by The Gallery Mourmans, The Netherlands
BabyBoop Bowls. 2001 [bottom left]
Stainless steel
Three bowls: 1⅝ × 9 × 7⅝" (4 × 23 × 19.5 cm), 1⅝ × 9 × 7⅞" (4 × 23 × 20 cm),
and 1⅝ × 11⁷⁄₁₆ × 8⅛" (4 × 29 × 21 cm)
Manufactured by Alessi SpA, Italy

Sketch for Blown Out Of Proportion (B.O.O.P.) (1998). N.d. [top right]
BabyBoop Vase. 2001 [center right]
Stainless steel
11¹³⁄₁₆ × 8⅞ × 4½" (30 × 22.5 × 11.5 cm)
Manufactured by Alessi SpA, Italy
Sketch for BabyBoop Vase (2001). N.d. [bottom right]

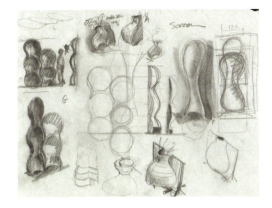

B.O.O.P.

The piece that began the Blown Out Of Proportion (B.O.O.P.) collection was a large vase that, in typical Arad fashion, was inspired by the discovery of a new technology with great expressive potential: superplastic aluminum formed into hollows using a cavity-forming process. Some fine-grained ceramics and metals can be made superplastic, which allows them to be stretched well beyond their normal breaking points, and cavity-forming involves heating and inflating a thin sheet of that aluminum through a stencil and into a cavity—rather than against a mold. Arad used the forms resulting from bubbles of aluminum to make billowy vases and tables, which later inspired a series of bowls manufactured by Alessi.

Blown Out Of Proportion (B.O.O.P.) Vase. 1998 [right]
Superplastic aluminum
7' 8" × 59½" × 15" (233.7 × 151.1 × 38.1 cm)
Edition by The Gallery Mourmans, The Netherlands
Sketch for Blown Out Of Proportion (B.O.O.P.) (1998). N.d.
[top & bottom left]

Bodyguards>

The Bodyguards, a recent result of Arad's experiments with blown aluminum, are all derived from the same bulbous shape, intersected and carved in various ways. Although Arad had sworn off designing rocking chairs, it seemed a natural application for this new technology, allowing him to create these large, polished pieces, which, in addition to rocking back and forth, also swivel in a way Arad describes as "omnidirectional." With the Bodyguards, as with much of his furniture, Arad explores the expressive qualities of the material, pursuing a way to transcend its physical limitations. He has described the pieces as monsters—huge and labor intensive, some resembling a human torso and revealing colorful insides when cut. (Arad was teased about the number of security guards present at a show in Dolce & Gabbana's Metropol space in Milan, in 2006—hence the name.)

Konx. 1999 [above]
Molded float glass and stainless steel
13×47¼×31½" (33×120×80 cm)
Manufactured by Fiam Italia SpA, Italy

Bodyguard. 2007 [opposite, top]
Polished and partially colored superplastic aluminum
Dimensions unknown
Edition by The Gallery Mourmans, The Netherlands
Bodyguard nº4. 2007 [opposite, bottom left]
Polished and patinated superplastic aluminum
6' 2"×43"×46" (188×109.2×116.8 cm)
Edition by The Gallery Mourmans, The Netherlands

Bodyguard nº5. 2007 [bottom right]
Polished and partially colored superplastic aluminum
49×36×70½" (124.5×91.4×179.1 cm)
Edition by The Gallery Mourmans, The Netherlands

Bodyguard nº3. 2007
Polished and partially colored superplastic aluminum
67×33×53" (170.2×83.8×134.6 cm)
Edition by The Gallery Mourmans, The Netherlands

Les Diablerets

The ski station Les Diablerets, with its spectacular views of the Western Alps, sits at the summit of a glacier 9,800 feet above sea level, called Glacier 3000, close to the border between the French and Swiss Alps. Arad designed a rotating restaurant for the very peak of the glacier, just above an existing building by Swiss architect Mario Botta, which marks the terminus of the highest gondola. In Arad's scheme, the new building is accessed by an escalator that rotates along with the restaurant, meeting at intervals with Botta's building for safe and covered passage. The restaurant provides spectacular views and the thrill of feeling just barely balanced on the very top of the Alps.

Panoramic Restaurant at Les Diablerets, Gstaad. Project. 2007

∧Upperworld Hotel

The Battersea Power Station is one of London's most prominent and iconic landmarks and is therefore difficult to convert to new use. Arad was invited by Parkview, a developer, to design a luxury hotel atop an equally ambitious redevelopment by Grimshaw Architects. The hotel sits within Battersea's four famous chimneys, and its layout features a double spine of horizontal tubular passages linked at the ends by two autonomous hubs. The northern hub holds the hotel's reception area, bar, restaurant, and function rooms, and the southern hub holds facilities open to the public. The lower tube also contains an automated shuttle that transports guests to their rooms. The project shown here stalled on the drawing board when the complex plans for redevelopment encountered several obstacles—not least an engineering analysis that found the chimneys structurally unsound and, to the dismay of the public, proposed tearing them down.

Upperworld Hotel, Battersea Power Station, London. Project. 2003

Reinventing the Wheel∧

Reinventing the Wheel continues the shelving revolution that Arad began with Bookworm (pages 60–63), This Mortal Coil, and One Way or Another (pages 58–59). Inspired by a children's toy featuring a small globe floating inside a sphere, Arad designed a bookcase with a wheel-within-a-wheel construction that can easily be rolled around, with the shelves remaining level and books and other objects safely supported.

Reinventing the Wheel (RTW). 1996 [bottom]
Patinated steel and anodized aluminum
D. 14" (35.6 cm), diam. 51³⁄₁₆" (130 cm)
Edition by Ron Arad Studio, Italy
Sketch for Reinventing the Wheel (RTW) (1996). N.d. [top]

Restless. 2007 [opposite]
Polished stainless steel and patinated steel
6' 2" × 8' 1" × 17" (188 × 246.4 × 43.2 cm)
Edition by Ron Arad Associates, London

Infinity. 1999 [above]
Extruded polypropylene
Each 3¾ × 2¼ × 5¾" (9.5 × 5.7 × 14.5 cm)
Manufactured by Kartell, Italy

Apartment in Place des Vosges, Paris. 2007
Interior design of kitchen, staircase, and mezzanine

Swarovski Hotel, Wattens, Austria. Project. 2004

<∧Chalk Farm Road Studio

Eight years after founding One Off, his studio in Covent Garden, Arad and his partner, Caroline Thorman, founded Ron Arad Associates in an old shed on Chalk Farm Road, just north of London's Camden Town. (One Off would be incorporated into this new company in 1993.) With the studio now operating as its own client, Arad—never keen on working for other people—was free to design the space as a projection of his own idea of what design is: a creative process naturally flowing between different scales (from objects to buildings) and techniques (from advanced to handcrafted and ancestral). It is characterized by a landscaped floor, punctuated with structural columns calligraphic in appearance, that demarcates areas for a showroom, design office, and workshop. Like the floor, the trans-lucent PVC roof undulates with a structure of steel ribs and mesh ceiling. The windows are also made of PVC, and are large enough to bring plenty of light into the split-level space.

Chalk Farm Road Studio, Ron Arad Associates, London. 1989–91
[previous page & above]

Dobrininsky, Moscow. 2007
Design for interior sculpture, landscape, restaurant, and bar in
commercial building

^Misfits

Misfits is a seating system Arad developed, at Patrizia Moroso's request, to launch Waterlily, a new water-blown foam made by ICI Polyurethane. From large cubes of foam he carved out modular—or, rather, mock-modular—sections, intending them to be graciously ill-fitting with each other (hence the name). The modules can stand on their own or be combined in various ways, but however they are lined up they are meant to look deliberately mismatched, without continuity from section to section. Some sections have backs and some do not, and the irregular solids and voids created quite a challenge for Moroso, who had to figure out how to cover them all with fabric. The recent reedition of Misfits is made with slightly larger blocks from a different polyurethane foam, which is injected into a mold rather than cut.

Paved with Good Intentions>

Arad's installation for Design Miami in 2005 consisted of sixty-nine tables made of mirror-polished stainless steel and covering an entire gallery, folding at the corners and climbing up the walls like handsome quicksilver parasites from outer space. Arad had experimented with reflective tables eleven years earlier, in an installation for one of the Fondation Cartier's famous Soirées Nomades, in which designers were invited to provide a stage for music and other types of performances in Jean Nouvel's building for the Paris-based foundation. There, Arad displayed forty tables that covered the ground floor, reflecting the surrounding trees and enhancing the glass architecture's openness toward the city surrounding it.

Misfits. 1993 [top]
Injected flame-retardant polyurethane foam, steel, polypropylene, and wool
Six modules: each h. variable, base 39⅜ × 39⅜" (100 × 100 cm)
Manufactured by Moroso SpA, Italy, 2007
Sketch for Misfits (2007). N.d. [bottom]

Paved with Good Intentions. 2005 [left]
Installation at Art Basel Miami, 2005
Paved with Good Intentions Table nº48. 2005 [top right]
Mirror-polished, laser-cut stainless steel
55"×8' 2"×15" (139.7×238.8×38.1 cm)
Edition by Ron Arad for The Gallery Mourmans, The Netherlands

Paved with Good Intentions Low Table nº34. 2005 [bottom right]
Mirror-polished, laser-cut stainless steel
8' 7 ¹⁵⁄₁₆" ×7' 10 ⅞" ×47 ¼" (264×241×120 cm)
Edition by Ron Arad for The Gallery Mourmans, The Netherlands

FIG 1 Khashayar Naimanan. Design Products Action Figure (Ron Arad Action Figure). 2001. Resin, card, and polystyrene, 13 3/8 × 10 5/8 × 3 15/16" (34 × 27 × 10 cm). Edition by Khashayar Naimanan and Chris Fitzgerald

NO DISCIPLINE: RON ARAD AT THE ROYAL COLLEGE OF ART

PAOLA ANTONELLI

Design as a discipline is often defined, by default, in juxtaposition with other, bordering fields: it is not Art because it cannot be only about self-expression; it is not Architecture because the context and the scale are different; it is not Craft because it tinkers with mass-production tools; it is not Engineering because it reaches far beyond functional soundness. Designers often find themselves defining their work's relationship with the market, with technology, or with history—in other words, with the world—by linking it with other, more established practices. Individuals who break this mold tend to become, for other designers, role models symbolizing freedom and emancipation.

That is why for many designers Ron Arad is a hero—a notion that he would be quick to dismiss with a shrug, even though his hat-T-shirt-baggy-pants superhero costume might be proof enough. "MY FIRST SIGHTING OF RON ARAD WAS IN THE GRAND HALL OF PADDINGTON STATION, IN LONDON. THIS WAS PROBABLY IN 2002, OR THEREABOUTS. I NOTICED HIS HAT AND BAGGY ORANGE TROUSERS." Max Lamb, class of 2006 (<FIG 1) Like Bruno Munari, Shiro Kuramata, and Ettore Sottsass before him, he has nimbly jumped crevasses and flown over tall buildings, creating bridges and pulverizing walls with his disregard for definitions and his

omnivorous curiosity for all fields of human creativity. His accomplishment over the past three decades, in the culture of design as well as in design itself, "RON IS A CULTURE GENERATOR." Assa Ashuach, class of 2003 (FIG 2>>) has been to stir up the design world by repeatedly updating the figure of the architect/designer/artist, repositioning design side by side with art, both in discourse and in the market, all the while also keeping a foot firmly in industrial production and large-scale distribution. He has reinvigorated the old-fashioned practice of sketching and drawing by hand while adopting the most advanced drafting and visualization software. He has played a major role in establishing conceptual design—possibly the field's most promising new trajectory, with its examination of social behaviors and the relationship between technology and everyday life—marrying it to hefty doses of crafty hands-on experimentation to give it worldly substance. He has resuscitated tired furniture-design staples—he is a serial chairer—while at the same time diving into the most innovative technologies, reinventing known typologies and inventing new archetypes. "THERE WERE MY PRE-RCA DAYS, WHEN I MADE SOFAS AND CHAIRS THAT GENERALLY COLLAPSED. SINCE GOING TO THE RCA I HAVEN'T MADE A SINGLE PIECE OF FURNITURE, AND FEWER PEOPLE HAVE BEEN INJURED AS A RESULT." Jimmy Loizeau, class of 2001, Design Interactions tutor (FIG 3>>) In sum, he has celebrated curiosity and intellectual restlessness and has done so with a devil-may-care attitude that is the trait that perhaps most inspires designers looking for someone, anyone, to make their day: Arad appears to be free, and in his freedom, even more than in his boundless talent, resides his power and distinction. Arad is well known as a maverick and iconoclast; "WHEN I MET HIM HE WAS MUCH BIGGER. HE LOOKED LIKE A BADDIE OFF 24 BUT WITH A MISCHIEVOUS GLINT IN HIS EYE" James Auger, class of 2001, Design Interactions tutor (FIG 3>>) with his disregard for disciplines—and (at least apparently) also for discipline—he has defined much of the current panorama of design, inspiring a generation of practitioners who disregard established modes of practice in favor of mutant design careers that are flexible enough to encompass the range of contemporary design applications, from interactions and interfaces to furniture and shoes. "I CAME FROM A DIFFERENT DISCIPLINE, VISUAL COMMUNICATION, AND I WAS WELCOMED BY RON—AS WAS A GIRL WHO HAD ONLY MADE SHOES, AND A DOCTOR!" Matthias Megyeri, class of 2003 But Arad's impact on design's trajectory is also due to the chain reaction he has initiated at London's Royal College of Art, where he has been head of the Department of Design Products since 1997: an extraordinary community of highly diverse and unconventional designers and thinkers, each hand-picked for his or her intellectual peculiarities, potential, and individualism "FOR SOME NEVER-DISCLOSED REASON, HE ALWAYS SKETCHES PORTRAITS OF THE STUDENTS

WHO ATTEND THE INTERVIEWS." Marloes ten Bhömer, class of 2003 (FIG 4>>) "THE FIRST TIME WE SAW RON WAS PROBABLY AT THE INTERVIEW FOR THE RCA. RON WAS SITTING THERE DRAWING DOODLES OF US, THE INTERVIEWEES." Shay Alkalay and Yael Mer, class of 2006 (and all of them finishing the program even more idiosyncratic and opinionated than they were at the start), who are now in turn defining the meaning and the role of design.[1] Although (rather interestingly) none of them is an Arad clone, they all share—in addition to the great design talent required for admission in the first place—finely honed critical skills, an exceptional curiosity about innovation, and a certain swagger: a combination of traits guaranteed to move design toward new models for living in the contemporary world. Whether examining environmental responsibility or the acknowledgment of death's inevitability, whether marrying a new technology with civil disobedience or designing a new bike for children with disabilities, the projects designed by RCA students under Arad have been both sure-footed and experimental. "I'D SAY RON IS VERY CRITICAL. IF YOU ARE REALLY BAD, HE ARGUES ABOUT AND CRITICIZES EVERYTHING YOU DO. IF YOU ARE REALLY GOOD, HE ARGUES ABOUT AND CRITICIZES EVERYTHING YOU DO. IF YOU DON'T GET A RESPONSE, IT'S BECAUSE YOU ARE NOT INTERESTING." Max Lamb, class of 2006

DESIGN AND SCHOOLS

In the past thirty years design schools have become the most important centers for the production of ideas, overtaking the research and development departments of corporations and think tanks and shifting the focus from the production of finite artifacts to a more conceptual brand of experimentation. The progress of design education is a fascinating and rather unexplored subject, at least partly because of design's constantly changing definition, which always requires a modifier—graphic, furniture, automotive, or fashion. Moreover, schools entirely devoted to design are quite rare; it is far more likely for design to be limited to a division of an art or polytechnical school. "WHEN I WAS AT THE RCA, IT WAS THE END OF AN ERA. ALL THE STUDENTS WERE DESPERATE FOR SOMEONE INSPIRING. WHEN THE RUMOR STARTED THAT RON MIGHT TAKE THE JOB, EVERYONE WAS THRILLED—BUT I WAS ENVIOUS OF THE FIRST-YEAR STUDENTS WHO WOULD GET THE OPPORTUNITY." Roberto Feo, class of 1997, Platform 10 tutor

Since the second half of the nineteenth century, different design schools have reached influential and creative zeniths at different times, each becoming the beacon of international design for the period. This dynamic has closely followed social, economic, and political history: certain schools blossomed under enlightened patronage, or in collaboration with receptive industries, or when inspired and defined by crucial political circumstances. Each high moment also coincided with the tenure of truly visionary educators (in some cases practicing architects or designers) and sometimes with the construction of new buildings to celebrate fervor and intellectual splendor, or the formation of new departments to mark the arrival of a new intellectual moment. "AN EDUCATOR? THAT CONJURES IMAGES OF A BLACK CLOAK, MORTARBOARD, AND STICK! WELL, HE'S GOT THE HAT." Peter Marigold, class of 2006 (FIG 5>)

Among such prominent schools and periods are the Glasgow School of Art, where, at the end of the nineteenth century, Director Francis Newberry commissioned from alumnus Charles Rennie Mackintosh the building that would ground the Arts and Crafts movement in history; Moscow's Vkhutemas (an acronym for Vysshie Khudozhestvenno-Tekhnicheskie Masterskie, or Higher Technical-Artistic Studios), founded in 1918 and so named in 1920, where the most important practitioners of Constructivism and Suprematism, from El Lissitzky to Aleksandr Rodchenko, Kazimir Malevich, and Vladimir Tatlin, studied or taught; and the Bauhaus (perhaps the best-known example) founded by Walter Gropius in Weimar in 1919 to gather all the arts under modernism, and subsequently closed by the Nazis in 1933. The Cranbrook Academy of Art, near Detroit, was founded in 1925 by the newspaper publisher George G. Booth and his wife Ellen Scripps Booth, who commissioned Finnish architect Eliel Saarinen to design an institution modeled after the most progressive examples of European design education, including the Arts and Crafts movement and the Bauhaus; in the 1950s Cranbrook became the cradle for a glorious decade of American design, with alumni and teachers including Charles Eames and Eero Saarinen, Eliel's son. In the 1930s schools were influenced by the idea, brought to the United States by the many European émigrés associated with the Bauhaus, of unity among the arts and interdisciplinary liberal studies. One such school was Black Mountain College, founded in 1933 in North Carolina, which not only became Josef and Anni Albers's new home but was also a vibrant melting pot where the likes of Buckminster Fuller, Merce Cunningham, John Cage, Gropius, and many others all taught together. In 1937 László Moholy-Nagy, who had taught the Bauhaus's preliminary course since 1923, was invited by Walter Paepcke, the design-enlightened chairman of Container Corporation of America, to found the New Bauhaus in Chicago. The school lasted only one year.

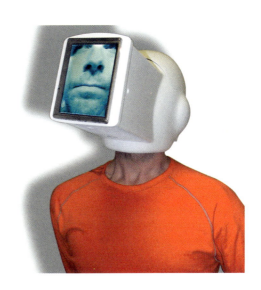

FIG 2 Assa Ashuach.
"My Trousers" (trousers you
can walk and sit with). 2002.
Denim, aluminum, plywood,
and polyester fabric,
39⅜ × 15¾ × 9¹³/₁₆"
(100 × 40 × 25 cm).
Edition by Assa Ashuach Studio,
London

FIG 3 James Auger
and Jimmy Loizeau.
Interstitial Space Helmet (ISH).
2004. Polycarbonato
and electronic media,
8⅝ × 11¾ × 17¾"
(22 × 30 × 45 cm)

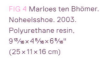

FIG 4 Marloes ten Bhömer.
Noheelsshoe. 2003.
Polyurethane resin,
9¹³/₁₆ × 4⁵/₁₆ × 6⁵/₁₆"
(25 × 11 × 16 cm)

FIG 5 Peter Marigold. PROP. 2006.
Reclaimed Madagascan
mahogany from the British
Museum collection, metal,
and bag of rice,
PROP: 1 × 3¹⁵/₁₆ × 43⁵/₁₆"
(2.5 × 10 × 110 cm);
installation dimensions variable

In the second half of the twentieth century, as the various design professions became more specialized, the schools followed suit, naturally choosing nearby industries and their faculty's core interests as centers of gravity. Some became reluctant design schools, as did the polytechnic universities in Milan and Turin immediately after World War II, producing legendary but unemployed architects—Achille, Pier Giacomo, and Livio Castiglioni; Gae Aulenti; Marco Zanuso; and Sottsass, to name just a few—who fortuitously met equally legendary and forward-looking industrial manufacturers—Cassina, Zanotta, and Arflex, for instance—in search of products. In the background, the mechanical and chemical industries were brimming with innovations waiting to be applied; together, the designers and manufacturers established a formula for collaboration, based on sharing technical knowledge, dreams, and goals, that later bore fruit in the 1960s.

Other schools whose identities were defined by relationships with industrial producers include the Hochschule für Gestaltung, in Ulm, Germany, founded in 1953 and considered by many to be the continuation of the Bauhaus (Josef Albers was a visiting teacher, as was Johannes Itten, the painter who had developed the Bauhaus's preliminary course), which forged German industrial design by linking directly with companies such as Braun and Lufthansa. Pasadena's Art Center College of Design, founded in 1930 by advertising executive Edward A. Adams, focuses on automotive and visual design and counts among its graduates design directors and chief creative officers at BMW and Ford, as well as renowned film directors.[2] Some design schools were begun by entrepreneurs as incubators of talent for their own companies and then acquired a life of their own, as did the California Institute of the Arts (CalArts), which was founded by Walt and Roy Disney in 1961.

The cultural tidal wave of the late 1960s put politics front and center in art, architecture, and design schools, and in the 1970s an intense debate about design's responsibility toward consumerist society—especially during the energy crises and the years of terrorism in Europe—led many designers to embrace new forms of expression, including music and performance. The Rhode Island School of Design was one such site of intense contamination, where art and design mixed with a thriving music culture in the 1970s and '80s, producing such alumni as fashion designer Nicole Miller and two members of the Talking Heads.

As these militant designers from the late 1960s and '70s became teachers, they brought their politics and aesthetics to bear on the programs in which they taught. Milan's Domus Academy was founded in 1982 by Maria Grazia Mazzocchi, daughter of the founder and publisher of *Domus* magazine. The academy, under Andrea Branzi's direction in the 1980s, became the educational arm of the radical design that had evolved in Italy in the 1970s, ushering in an approach that merged poetic and conceptual design with advanced technology.

Some design schools, like the Royal College of Art, were established by national governments, often in a period when design embodied cultural pride and economic promise, or were later supported or adopted by the government, as was Finland's Veistokoulu (School of Arts and Crafts), founded in 1871, which eventually became the state-run Taideteollinen korkeakoulu (University of Art and Design).[3] In the 1980s President François Mitterand aspired to make Paris into the world capital of innovative architecture with the Grands Travaux, a publicly funded architectural program of remarkable breadth, impact, and arrogance that included, among other buildings, the Science Museum in Parc de la Villette and the Bibliothèque nationale de France. Jack Lang, at the time France's minister of culture, made a mighty effort to establish French culture throughout the world, and one result was ENSCI/Les Ateliers (École nationale supérieure de création industrielle), founded in 1982. Les Ateliers has produced some of the most interesting French designers active today, such as Patrick Jouin, Matali Crasset, Inga Sempé, and Mathieu Lehanneur.

In the late 1980s, when computers started to enter every aspect of daily life, some schools that had begun as encounters of art and technology became centers for the study of the communication between human beings and machines, examining how design facilitates and explains this relationship. The Massachusetts Institute of Technology's Media Lab, founded by Nicholas Negroponte and MIT President Jerome Wiesner in 1980, has been home to a number of influential teachers, such as Muriel Cooper, Hiroshi Ishii, and John Maeda, who established information and interaction design as disciplines to be reckoned with.

In the past decade design has turned another corner, this one created by the palpable urgency of economic, environmental, political, and demographic crises, all made more vivid by new technologies. This coupling of world events and technology has generated a new awareness of the eternal human condition,

"MOSTLY WE LEARNED TO DEFINE OUR OWN TERRITORIES WITHIN THE DESIGN FIELD." Shay Alkalay and Yael Mer, class of 2006

resulting in the refocusing of design pedagogy toward more humanistic—rather then object-centered—goals, such as in a course called "Man and Humanity,"

FIG 6 Troika (Eva Rucki, Conny Freyer, and Sebastien Noel). SMS Guerrila Projector. 2003. Aluminum, 13¾ × 3¹⁵⁄₁₆ × 3¹⁵⁄₁₆" (35 × 10 × 10 cm)

FIG 8 Ben Wilson. Tilting Trike. 2002. Aluminum, stainless steel, mild steel, and rubber, 23⅝ × 43⁵⁄₁₆ × 35⁷⁄₁₆" (60 × 110 × 90 cm)

FIG 7 rAndom international (Hannes Koch, Florian Ortkrass, and Stuart Wood). Instant Labelling Tape. 2004. Adhesive tape, two sizes: h. 2" (5.1 cm), diam. of roll 4" (10.2 cm); and h. ¾" (1.9 cm), diam. of roll 2¼" (5.7 cm). Manufactured by Suck UK Ltd., United Kingdom

FIG 9 Julie Mathias and Michael Cross. "Flood" Light. 2004. Water and electricity, h. 35⁷⁄₁₆" (90 cm), diam. 7⅞" (20 cm). Manufactured by WOKmedia

FIG 10 Paul Cocksedge. Crystallize. 2005. Swarovski crystals, laser module, and glass, h. variable, from 35⁷⁄₁₆" (90 cm) to 70⅞" (180 cm). Manufactured by Paul Cocksedge Studio for Swarovski Crystal Palace

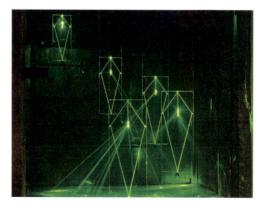

on design for humanitarian needs, at the Eindhoven Design Academy. Today's most interesting schools are those that combine a strong philosophy and a loose structure, encouraging interdisciplinary study, experimentation, and collaboration with other fields; one such institution is the Royal College of Art. "I THINK THAT RON'S VIRTUE IS THAT HE HAS IDENTIFIED THAT DESIGN'S AREA OF INTEREST IS EXPANDING, AND HE ALLOWS PEOPLE TO EXPLORE AREAS THAT HAVE NOT TRADITIONALLY FALLEN INTO WHAT WE UNDERSTAND AS INDUSTRIAL DESIGN." Roberto Feo, class of 1997, Platform 10 tutor

THE ROYAL COLLEGE OF ART

The Royal College of Art comprises six schools (Applied Art, Architecture and Design, Communications, Fashion and Textiles, Fine Art, and Humanities) and nineteen academic departments within those schools ranging from traditional specializations such as painting, conservation, photography, and architecture to new departments such as Design Interactions and Design Products (these latter two will introduce us to Arad's influence on the curriculum). More than eight hundred students are taught by one hundred teachers, most of them renowned practitioners in their fields. The fact that the RCA is a postgraduate school certainly contributes to its stellar record, as does the echo created by alumni like David Hockney, Tracey Emin, Ridley Scott, and Jake and Dinos Chapman, in the arts; Philip Treacy and Zandra Rhodes, in fashion; and Alan Fletcher, Jonathan Barnbrook, James Dyson, Jasper Morrison, Tim Brown, Ross Lovegrove, Fiona Raby and Tony Dunne, Tord Boontje, Thomas Heatherwick, and Ineke Hans, among many, many others, in architecture and design. "I ORIGINALLY WANTED TO JOIN THE DESIGN INTERACTION DEPARTMENT, BUT I DIDN'T THINK I WAS INTELLIGENT ENOUGH. THEN, AT ONE OF THE DESIGN PRODUCTS SHOWS, I SAW THIS GUN THAT SHOT SMS MESSAGES, AND THE PROGRAM LOOKED LIKE IT COULD BE FOR ME." Peter Marigold, class of 2006 (<<FIG 5)

Design in the United Kingdom has for centuries been part of a charged relationship between craft and industry. In the eighteenth century Josiah Wedgwood separated the production facilities for his ceramic wares into two locations, one factory for low-end, large-number series, and another for smaller, more precious editions—thus introducing the distinction between mass and limited production. In the second half of the nineteenth century, at the height of the Industrial Revolution, William Morris and other protagonists of the Arts and Crafts movement separated industrial manufacturing from "good" design, embracing an ethics in which the craftsman—independent maker of ideas, enlightened master of beauty and honesty—sat on one side of the spectrum, while the industrial manufacturer—actuator of the evil and the ugly, manipulating materials against their own nature—was on the other. Yet even in the nineteenth century, as it was in the 1960s and is today, the best of design was created in the intermediate stations between these poles, when creative tension is maintained between designer and manufacturer, technology and craftsmanship, with the resulting exchange of knowledge and wisdom harvested by designers and transformed into new, strange kinds of beauty.

The history of the RCA has reflected these changes in attitude toward industrial production. The school's first incarnation, the Government School of Design, set up in 1837 to train designers for industrial careers, was heavily influenced by London's Great Exhibition of 1851, organized by Sir Henry Cole and sponsored by Prince Albert and the Royal Society of Arts. The exhibition also led to the founding of the Victoria and Albert Museum, which was established by the British government in 1852 to house and display the contemporary objects that Cole had purchased.[4] This was a collection with a didactic imperative, intended to be an example for manufacturers and designers. Cole believed that a better education in the industrial arts would contribute to the well-being of the whole country (as such, the collection was controlled by England's Department of Education and Science until 1983) and counter the abundance of industrial products of bad taste and poor quality.[5] He reinforced the school's focus toward the industry and producing "works of art for the whole people."[6] Its first notable alumnus was Christopher Dresser, who began his studies there in 1847, when he was fifteen years old; in 1852 he became a student lecturer and began making an articulate and motivated case for the technical practice and knowledge that he deemed necessary to form designers for the industry.

In the twentieth century the RCA moved away from design and the decorative arts to concentrate on fine art. The school was pivotal in the development of modern British sculpture in the 1920s, with such students as Barbara Hepworth and Henry Moore, but maintained a relatively low profile until Robert Darwin became its head in 1948. Attuned to the humors of contemporary architects and designers, Darwin commissioned RCA instructors Hugh Casson, Robert Goodden, and H. T. Cadbury Brown to design a new building on Kensington Gore, an example of late British modernism that anticipated the Brutalist movement of the 1960s. The school moved in 1962 and still occupies what is now called the Darwin Building. "SURVIVAL OF THE MOST INTERESTING—AFTER ALL, WE WERE IN THE DARWIN BUILDING." Matthias Megyeri, class of 2003 Darwin renewed the RCA's ties to architecture and design, at the same time nurturing students such as Hockney and supporting a strong Pop art sensibility in the late 1950s and 1960s, and turned the school into an exclusively postgraduate institution in 1967.

The design curriculum followed various directions until the 1970s, when the courses of furniture and industrial design were divided into a solid and modernist Scandinavian tradition for the former, and an Ulm-like functionalism for the latter. Sir Christopher Frayling, who became the school's rector in 1996, remembers 1981 as the year that postmodernism arrived at the RCA, when Daniel Weil, a design student from Argentina, presented a deconstructed radio at the end-of-the-year show: "Famously, within a very traditional design culture, he did an exhibit of all those see-through radios hanging in a polythene tent, and he called it Homage to Duchamp. The examiners stood there and did not know what to make of it: was it art, was it design, was it culture, was it technical, they did not know what was going on.... That was the moment when postmodernism started here."[7] Weil went on to participate in the first show of the Memphis group, the Italian-based group considered the epitome of postmodernism, and became a partner in the design firm Pentagram shortly thereafter.

In the early to mid-1980s the school was home to a generation of talented students, including Morrison, Lovegrove, and Dunne, who defined an approach to industrial design based on experimentation, scenarios, concepts, research on materials and technologies, and altogether less attention paid to finished products. At the same time a separate Design Engineering department was addressing the traditional discipline of industrial design—of making things for industrial pro-duction. In keeping with its tradition of attention to the latest technologies, the school inaugurated, in 1990, a course dedicated to computer-related design.

ARAD AT THE RCA

Arad first came to the RCA in 1994, to teach a master class in furniture. Frayling introduced him to the class by showing a beer commercial made around that time that featured a designer throwing away a Memphis-style chair and replacing it with one that resembled Arad's Rover (pages 26–27). (Ah, a culture where design can sell beer; design in England is as public a topic as — perhaps not soccer, or the weather, but at least beer.) At the time Arad was a professor of product design at Vienna's Hochschule für angewandte Kunst, a position he would hold for three more years. "WE USED TO CALL HIM MASTER YODA, LIKE THE JEDI MASTER IN *STAR WARS* WHO SPEAKS IN THIS UNCANNY, MYSTERIOUS WAY. LIKE MANY OF THE TUTORS AT THE COLLEGE, RON IS A GUIDE RATHER THAN A TEACHER." Sebastien Noel, class of 2003 (<<FIG 6)

In 1997 Arad became head of the Furniture department at RCA; as the story goes, he was on the search committee that was looking for a new department head, but the committee ended up offering the job to him. At the time the Furniture department and the Industrial Design department were two separate divisions, and the absence of the word "design" after "furniture," Arad says, meant that it was "almost like running a craft course." Frayling and Arad lobbied to have them joined, and in 1998 Arad created a new division with a new name: Design Products.[8] "I REMEMBER RON EXPLAINING DESIGN PRODUCTS, INSTEAD OF PRODUCT DESIGN, MEANING THAT EVERYTHING CAN BE SEEN AS A PRODUCT, AND HE'D LIKE US TO APPROACH PRODUCTS AS SUCH — SO VERY FREETHINKING." Matthias Megyeri, class of 2003 This subtle change implied an important shift in focus, from physical things meant to enter the commercial system of the world — the meaning normally associated with the word "products" — to any concept, idea, or construction examined through a design process: "I WOULD THINK THAT HE DESIGNED THE DEGREE WITH THE SAME STYLE AND PHILOSOPHY AS ANY OF HIS PRODUCTS OR PROTOTYPES." Hannes Koch, class of 2004, Platform 8 tutor (<<FIG 7) the product is an idea first and foremost, supported by an object. (A few years later, Dunne made a similar correction to the Computer-Related Design department, which became Design Interactions.)

It was indeed a momentous shift, and some industrial designers from the establishment found it quite traumatic. This was only the first of the lessons Arad carried over from the Architectural Association, the school he had attended in the 1970s.

ARAD AT THE AA

After a year of art school, at Jerusalem's Bezalel Academy, Arad moved to London in 1973. At that time the Architectural Association, directed by the charismatic Alvin Boyarsky, was a lively forum for the most interesting, disparate, autonomous, and atypical approaches to architecture—a period, according to one critic, when what seemed to be a laissez-faire attitude was actually generating groundbreaking culture:

> Pre-1968 optimistic modernism was being abandoned amid economic uncertainty and cultural conservatism. In architecture, too, democratic modernism was perceived to have failed and there was a swing towards historicist post-modernism and conservation. The AA's theorists did the opposite. They rejected kitsch post-modernism to become still more modernist. Like snakes shedding their skins, they discarded the failed utopian projects of "first" modernism to think up a new modernism with a more sophisticated idea of history and human identity, an architecture embodying modernity's chaos and disjuncture in its very shape.[9]

Arad recalls his interview and somewhat backhanded admission to the AA:

> I joined the queue for the interview. Alvin [Boyarsky] was there… looking at huge portfolios. I didn't have a portfolio. I walked into the room, and they asked me, "Why do you want to be an architect?" And I said, "I don't want to be an architect. My mother wants me to be an architect." Which was true, because she was worried that I might want to be an artist instead, and architecture is more respectable and safer. "Let's see your portfolio." I said, "I don't have one, but I have a pencil here. What do you want me to do?" I was cocky and stupid. And the same day after my interview, it was election night in London and it was a party, and some guy from the panel said to me, "Don't do it again. Don't go to your interview like that. We decided to give you a place, but it was a big argument and you nearly didn't get in." I was a reluctant architect most of the time at the AA. "YOU CAN CLEARLY SEE HIS STAMP AT THE RCA. HE'S INTENSE, ICONOCLASTIC, GENEROUS, FORWARD-LOOKING, AND HAS A GREAT BUSINESS SENSE." Sebastien Noel, class of 2003 (<<FIG 6)

Boyarsky, Arad says, was "pluralist to the point of being indifferent…. You could never know what he really thought." He had established a teaching system based on units, inspred by the eight autonomous *Unités pédagogiques d'architecture* that the French government had set up after the student strikes and riots of May 1968.[10] A unit could focus on anything that the instructor (called a "unit master") wanted, creating a school that was diverse and continuously changing, collegial but competitive. "RON IS OPEN-MINDED AND ACTUALLY ABLE TO GET INSIDE YOUR HEAD." Kelly Sant, class of 2001 There were cliques, there were star teachers and star students, there was brilliance and rivalry. Above all there was a comfortably dangerous atmosphere of anarchy and freedom that was the perfect turf for visionary ideas.

At that time unit masters like Rem Koolhaas were tutoring students like Zaha Hadid, and students like Hadid, Nigel Coates (the current head of the Architecture department at the RCA), and Peter Wilson would become unit masters as soon as they finished their degrees—"also a good way to balance the books," Arad adds. "I WAS INCREDIBLY LUCKY: MY TUTORS WERE MICHAEL MARRIOTT, TORD BOONTJE, AND JASPER MORRISON." Ben Wilson, class of 2001 (<<FIG 8) Arad remembers debates between Peter Cook, "who represented the decadence of architecture," and Brian Anson, fired by what Robin Middleton called his "posse of revolutionaries."[11] He also remembers Tony Dugdale's unit called "Towards Old-Time Architecture," and Mark Fisher's ironic "The Nice Ideas Unit." (Fisher later designed some of the most memorable rock concerts in history, for Pink Floyd, U2, and the Rolling Stones, among others; he remembers Arad as an "outstanding student," which would no doubt irritate Arad).[12] Bernard Tschumi was also at the AA, working toward a new era of conceptual architecture, in which the ideas informing a project were more important than a finished building. "RON SAID THAT WHEN HE DOES A PROTOTYPE HE TREATS IT LIKE IT IS GOING TO BE THE FINISHED PIECE." Dominic Wilcox, class of 2002 (FIG 11>>)

THE PLATFORMS
"THE DESIGN PRODUCTS DEPARTMENT WAS A BIG DESIGN PROJECT FOR RON. IN THE SYSTEM HE DESIGNED, STUDENTS ARE EMPOWERED. TUTORS HAVE TO PITCH TO THEM AT THE START OF EVERY YEAR, AND THE MOST RELEVANT AND INTERESTING IDEAS WIN STUDENTS. THE TUTORS ARE SUCCESSFUL, INTERESTING DESIGN PROFESSIONALS WHO CONSTANTLY CHALLENGE AND NEVER SAY THEY'RE HAPPY WITH YOUR WORK—IT COULD ALWAYS BE BETTER! NEITHER STUDENTS NOR TUTORS FEEL SAFE OR COMFORTABLE. THE STUDENTS ARE PASSIONATE PEOPLE FROM DIFFERENT EDUCATIONAL BACKGROUNDS AND CULTURES." Jane ní Dhulchaointigh, class of 2004

"Pluralism" remains one of Arad's favorite words, and it is one of the ideas that he brought with him to the RCA, in the form of platforms. "THERE WERE NO RESTRICTIONS IMPOSED, BUT ONE HAD TO JUSTIFY ONE'S IDEAS." Ben Wilson, class of 2001 (<<FIG 8)

When he merged the Furniture and Industrial Design departments, Arad also set into motion a teaching system based on autonomous units—like those at the AA, but now called "platforms"—to encourage different interests and directions, and he assigned each platform to the strongest and most opinionated tutors he could find. Proceeding on the assumption that graduate students know what they want to do, Arad feels that the platforms provide them with a sophisticated and competitive intellectual and technological trampoline. "ALMOST EVERYBODY SAYS THAT THE BEST DAY IN YOUR LIFE IS THE BIRTH OF YOUR CHILD. HELL, NO! THE RCA WAS REALLY THE BEST TIME I HAD. I FOUND THE RCA SO MATURE, MULTICULTURAL, AND MULTIDISCIPLINARY THAT I USED TO COMPARE IT TO AN AIRPORT." Julie Mathias, class of 2004 (<<FIG 9) Dunne remembers his days as a platform leader, from 1998 to 2004:

> Leading a platform was a fantastic learning experience. I believe it is the best way to learn how to teach. You have to take full responsibility for your approach. You are thrown in at the deep end, have one day per week, twelve students, and five other highly competitive platforms to deal with. Each platform is like a mini-course, and you have to do nearly everything. The tutors are examined as much as the students, and in Platform 3 we always had a hard time, always had to defend what we did, always got grilled by the examiners. It really forced me to sharpen up what I was teaching and why our philosophy mattered…. Year after year examiners would question the validity of what we did, one year even wanting to fail our whole platform, and Ron would look at me and say, "Well…"—my cue to defend myself, again…. I couldn't afford to have an ounce of intellectual fat. Platform 3 was lean, mean, and always on the defensive![13] "I REALLY FELT QUITE NERVOUS AND EXCITED BY THE WHOLE COURSE. AT THE TIME IT FELT LIKE *STAR TREK* FOR DESIGN: GOING BOLDLY WHERE NO ONE HAD GONE BEFORE." Jimmy Loizeau, class of 2001, Design Interactions tutor (<<FIG 3)

Arad's freedom was guaranteed by Frayling and sealed by Hilary French, the program's deputy director, who has known Arad since the beginning of his career at the RCA. "I had complete freedom," Arad says. "I could bring Albert Speer and no one would complain." Among the tutors he brought to the program at the beginning were such brilliant designers as Morrison, Dunne, Michael Marriott, and Konstantin Grcic, and such promising curators and theoreticians as Daniel Charny; later he brought Tom Dixon, and even later Jurgen Bey and former students Noam Toran (FIG 13>), James Auger, Onkar Singh Kular (FIG 12>), and Roberto

FIG 11 Dominic Wilcox.
War Bowl. 2002. Plastic,
h. 5" (12.7 cm),
diam. 18" (45.7 cm).
Manufactured by
Thorsten van Elten

FIG 13 Onkar Kular.
Hari & Parker Spy Toys, In the
Science of Spying Project. 2007.
Plastic, with microphone and text-
messaging ears (Hari) and
CCTV nose and biometric paw
scanner (Parker),
Hari: 9¹³⁄₁₆ × 2¹⁵⁄₁₆ × 1⁹⁄₁₆"
(25×7.5×4 cm);
Parker: 6¹⁄₈ × 5¼ × 1⁹⁄₁₆"
(15.5×13.3×4 cm)

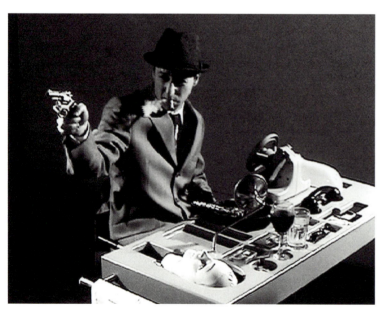

FIG 12 Noam Toran.
Object for Lonely Men. 2001.
Video (color, sound), 8:20

FIG 14 Tim Simpson.
Natural Deselection. 2006.
Mixed media, plants, and video,
installation
6' 6¾" × 6' 6¾" × 6' 6¾"
(200×200×200 cm)

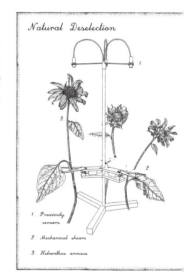

Feo. All of these tutors have busy careers in addition to teaching. "As a principle," Arad says, "I employ [at the RCA] only people who don't have time to teach." "WITH THE BOOKWORM, ARAD REINVENTED THE BOOKSHELF. WHEN HE ARRIVED AT THE RCA HE RECONFIGURED HOW THE STUDENTS WERE TAUGHT." Paul Cocksedge, class of 2002 (<<FIG 10) The students are selected, as is the tradition at the RCA, for their potential as much as — or even more than — for their previous work; Arad feels that the program is a place for mature students to become something more than problem-solvers or service-givers: "I always thought that in the course we take people that are totally and absolutely employable or in employment, and it takes us two years to make them unemployable, and I sort of mean it." "HIS INSTINCT ABOUT PEOPLE WAS TRULY AMAZING. HE WAS ABLE TO SEE WITHIN MINUTES WHAT KIND OF PERSON YOU WERE AND, MORE IMPORTANT, WHAT KIND OF CREATOR." Roger Arquer, class of 2005 "IN THE FIRST YEAR I GOT A REFERRAL — AN EXTRA-INTENSIVE TUTORIAL AT RON'S STUDIO, WHERE HE THEN TRIES TO UNTANGLE THE KNOT YOU'VE MADE FOR YOURSELF (DUE TO OVERENTHUSIASM WITH THE WEALTH OF INFORMATION OFFERED TO YOU IN THE FIRST YEAR)." Sarah van Gameren, class of 2007

Frayling agrees:

> He does actually have a quite strong philosophy, which is this kind of post-modernist idea of [acting] in a social world. Design is the creation of visual meaning in a responding context…. Also, he was completely at home with digital technology very early on. He has no religion, no formula; if you ask Ron what his philosophy is, he will say something very relativistic, like "A good designer is someone who fulfils his promise."[14] "RON WOULD REGULARLY SAY, 'IDEAS ARE CHEAP.' AT FIRST I DIDN'T KNOW WHAT HE MEANT, BUT GRADUALLY I REALIZED HE PROBABLY MEANT THAT THERE IS A BIG DIFFERENCE BETWEEN HAVING A GREAT IDEA AND ACTUALLY GETTING THAT IDEA MADE AND FINISHED IN A PRODUCT. IN THAT WAY, GREAT IDEAS DON'T HAVE MUCH VALUE UNTIL YOU DO SOMETHING WITH THEM." Dominic Wilcox, class of 2002 (<FIG 11)

The Frayling-Arad tenure coincided with design moving center stage both culturally and politically. The late 1990s saw the rise of the obnoxious and triumphant slogan "Cool Britannia," which celebrated the worldwide dominance of artists like Damien Hirst, bands like Oasis, architects like Norman Foster, and everything that came with being the beacon for all that was good and bad in visual and popular culture at that time. Cool Britannia was eagerly — and uncoolly — adopted by the British government to promote British culture, with the great quality and tradition of indigenous design among the reasons to be proud to be British. "When New Labor came in, in 1997," Frayling says, they were very keen to re-present Britain. I was involved with several government think tanks on how to emphasize the creative industry. We realized that… what we were strong at was design and design education…. We were trying to redefine the image of London, in particular…. The effect that it had on [the RCA] was that it made designers feel much more confident. They felt that society wanted them. When I first came to the College in the 1970s, a whole lot of designers were… sticking two fingers up at the world because they thought the world hated them, so they hated the world.[15]

Since Arad's arrival, the Design Products department has produced such diverse and innovative designers as Paul Cocksedge, Marloes ten Bhömer, Ben Wilson, Julie Mathias, Julia Lohmann, Dominic Wilcox, and Peter Marigold, among many others. (Their recollections of studying with Arad are excerpted in the quotes that accompany this essay, along with images of their work.)

"SOME THINGS THAT RON SAID THAT I LIKED A LOT AND THAT HELPED ME STEER MY WAY THROUGH MY DESIGN PRACTICE: 'DON'T WORRY, IT WILL NEVER BE YOUR LAST GOOD IDEA,' AND 'IF YOU DON'T CARE ABOUT MONEY, MONEY GETS JEALOUS'—A NICE THOUGHT WHEN YOU ARE REALLY STRUGGLING, TRYING TO SURVIVE IN SUPEREXPENSIVE LONDON WHILE DOING ONLY GOOD WORK THAT MAKES SENSE TO YOU AND THAT IS PURELY IDEALISTICALLY DRIVEN." Matthias Megyeri, class of 2003 According to French, one of Arad's most significant contributions to design culture is the establishment of the designer as author, as a full-fledged artist. Arad has created a community of such individualistic students and teachers, one that is as tight as it is loose, and as collegial as it is rife with controversy, much like that at Black Mountain College, which he considers an ideal school. Over the course of his tenure, and in tandem with his studio work, design objects have become art-market commodities—although he cannot bear to pronounce the words "art" and "design" together and in sequence—or moved into the realm of immaterial interactions. "WITH THE PRODUCT NOT STRICTLY FUNCTIONAL ANYMORE, WE ARE ALL LOOKING FOR DIFFERENT MEANINGS. IN THIS, RON IS A PIONEER." Sarah van Gameren, class of 2007 "So maybe I am a little bit to blame for this supply of people to Art Basel Miami, Design Miami/ Basel," he says. "They think they're following my footsteps by doing the Design Art thing, and I turn my back to it." "AFTER MY DEGREE I FELT LIKE A RACEHORSE BURSTING OUT OF THE STALLS." Tim Simpson, class of 2006 (<<FIG 14)

This attitude, which draws on the ancient, very effective stratagem of using polemics and provocation to elicit creative and energetic thought, is an example of the kind of counterintuitive qualities emulated by Arad's pupils and by many young designers around the world. In his celebration of pluralism and his open-mindedness toward students' inclinations—whether a contraption to cut and kill plants or a piece of furniture composed of a wooden box held up by a broomstick—Arad makes young designers believe in their own singular and peculiar reading of what a design practice should achieve and propose. Ron Arad has raised a generation of designers and myriad new possible directions for design. It is a great gift to the world.

[1] In June 2009, Ron Arad left his position at the RCA declaring, "Change is good." Unless otherwise noted, all quotes from Arad are taken from an interview with the author, New York, May, 21, 2008. The quotes from Arad's students are all taken from an interview with the author, conducted via e-mail in April and May of 2008.

[2] Among Art Center's graduates are the BMW Group's former Chief of Design Chris Bangle, Ford's Group Vice President of Design and Chief Creative Officer J Mays, and film director Michael Bay.

[3] On the history of the Veistokoulo, see http://www.taik.fi/taikista/tietoa_meista/historia.html (in Finnish). I am indebted to Nina Stritzler-Levine for her help on this topic.

[4] On the history of the Victoria and Albert Museum, see Anthony Burton, *Vision and Accident: The Story of the Victoria and Albert Museum* (London: V & A Publications, 1999); and Malcom Baker and Brenda Richardson, eds., *A Grand Design: The Art of the Victoria and Albert Museum* (London: V & A Publications; Baltimore: Baltimore Museum of Art, 1997).

[5] "In a few years, on a site opposite where the Exhibition stood, I hope we shall witness the foundation of an *Industrial University,* in the advantages of which all the nations of the world may equally share." Henry Cole, "Lecture on the International Results of the Exhibition of 1851, by Henry Cole," December 1, 1852, reprinted in *Fifty Years of Public Work of Sir Henry Cole, K.C.B.,* vol. 2 (London: George Bell and Sons, 1884), pp. 255–56.

[6] Cole, *What is Art Culture? An Address Delivered to the Manchester School of Art, 21st December 1877* (Manchester: G. Falkner & Son, 1877). Cole also founded *The Journal of Design and Manufactures,* the first monthly periodical devoted to design.

[7] Sir Christopher Frayling became rector of the RCA after teaching cultural history and tutoring in the Humanities department for twenty-three years. He will leave his post in summer 2009. Frayling, interview with the author, July 2, 2008.

[8] Of that important moment Frayling recalls, "The BBC was here at that time, filming a documentary about a year in the life of the College, a five-parter. So it all got filmed for posterity, the cameras were there.... The documentary was a big gamble, but it kind of positioned the College as the Oxford-Cambridge, the Oxbridge of design, which is what I wanted." Frayling interview, July 2, 2008.

[9] "Zaha Hadid," unsigned essay published by the Design Museum, London, and the British Council, http://www.designmuseum.org/design/zaha-hadid.

[10] Anthony Sutcliffe, *Paris: An Architectural History* (New Haven, Conn.: Yale University Press, 1993), p. 172.

[11] Robin Middleton, introduction to a lecture by Brian Anson, Columbia University, November 7, 2002. It is worth rendering the whole quote for its insight into the joining of design and politics: "Brian Anson took up the cudgels next at the Architectural Association, where he stoked up a posse of revolutionaries—many of them French refugees from the turmoils of 1968. Built form was of no account; it was politics that mattered. These were heady days, when architects still thought to have social concerns—things have changed. Unimaginably."

[12] "Ron was an outstanding student in the unit. His presence... was a result of the AA's then-current policy of not accepting mature students into the intermediate school without obliging them to complete the first-year course. At the end of his first year he moved on direct to the third year." Mark Fisher, e-mail to the author, July 8, 2008.

[13] Tony Dunne, e-mail to the author, April 9, 2008.

[14] Frayling interview, July 2, 2008.

[15] Ibid. Frayling explains the extent of his allegiance to Arad: "When I got knighted by the queen in the year 2000, for services to art and design education, my wife, Ellen, wore a Ron Arad hat to the palace." Moreover, Frayling, who is a Spaghetti-western fanatic and a passionate Clint Eastwood fan, chose as his motto *Perge scelus mihi diem perficias* (Latin for "Go ahead, punk, make my day!"); for his newly minted coat of arms he opted for the diagonal line that characterizes the illegitimate line of the family, highlighting the outlaw character of the research subjects that interest him. He was also chairman of the British Design Council in the late 1990s and early 2000s, and is currently chairman of the Arts Council.

^Millennium House

In 2001 Arad was commissioned to design a reception room and family dining room for the Millennium House in Doha, Qatar, the home of art collector Sheikh Saud Al-Thani, who had entrusted different parts of his residence to various art and design luminaries, including Achille Castiglioni, Marc Newson, and Philippe Starck (David Hockney was assigned the swimming pool). Like his colleagues, Arad was given carte blanche for this project—no restrictions, budget or otherwise, to guide or constrain him—so he proposed an ambitious and innovative design: a programmable, dynamic floor that could take the shape of a sofa, a table, or even an amphitheater, configuring itself in

a series of forms according to a set choreography, or freezing in a particular topography. Arad designed the floor like a three-dimensional pixel board operated by six hundred mechanical devices, each one activating a moveable tile to set the floor in motion. Arad experimented with several types of mechanisms, from hydraulic to pneumatic, until he decided the tiles would lift magnetically—a much quieter solution. The shifting landscape of the space is highlighted by large balls made of Tempur memory foam scattered throughout the room, rolling here and there as the floor shifts. The entire house project was shown at the Architecture Biennale, in Venice, in 2002.

Floor, Sheikh Saud Al-Thani's Millennium House, Doha, Qatar.
Project. 2001–2

Zion Square Sculpture ∧

In 2006 the Jerusalem Foundation and the Municipality of Jerusalem decided to revive Jaffa Road, one of the city's main arteries, and make it more appealing to, and comfortable for, pedestrians. Jaffa Road crosses Jerusalem from east to west, from the Old City all the way to downtown, forming many squares along the way; it is very crowded and popular, and as such it has been targeted by terrorists more than once and is often occupied by political protests. As part of a series of commissions for the redevelopment of these squares, Arad was invited to design a public sculpture for Zion Square, where Jaffa Road crosses Ben Yehuda Street downtown. The canopylike structure he proposed is made up of more than four hundred rectangular cells of various cross sections and lengths, all of them made of Cor-Ten steel lined with mirror-polished stainless steel. The sculpture's refractions and reflections of light are meant to be enhanced by the sun's movement across the sky throughout the day—the various ways it would hit the sculpture and the dynamic shadows that would result.

Zion Square Sculpture, Jerusalem. Project. 2006

Do-Lo-Res

Do-Lo-Res is a seating unit made of rectangular block elements, each one constructed from polyurethane foam, denser at the bottom and softer at the top. The name echoes the Lo-Rez-Dolores-Tabula-Rasa project (pages 198–99), and both designs are different manifestations of Arad's interest in digital pixilation and low resolution. Here the foam "pixels" of different heights are attached to a platform with steel pins and can be rearranged to create different sofa forms.

Do-Lo-Res. 2008
Polyurethane foam, polyester fibers, and wood
Dimensions variable
Manufactured by Moroso SpA, Italy

Design Museum
Holon

Arad's design for this museum in the city of Holon,
south of Tel Aviv, is dominated by five major bands of
undulating weatherproof steel, the curves of which
outline the museum's internal spaces. The bands act
as a defining design for the building, both supporting
it structurally and dictating its posture in relation to
its surroundings. The project is currently nearing
completion.

Design Museum Holon, Israel. 2004 – 9

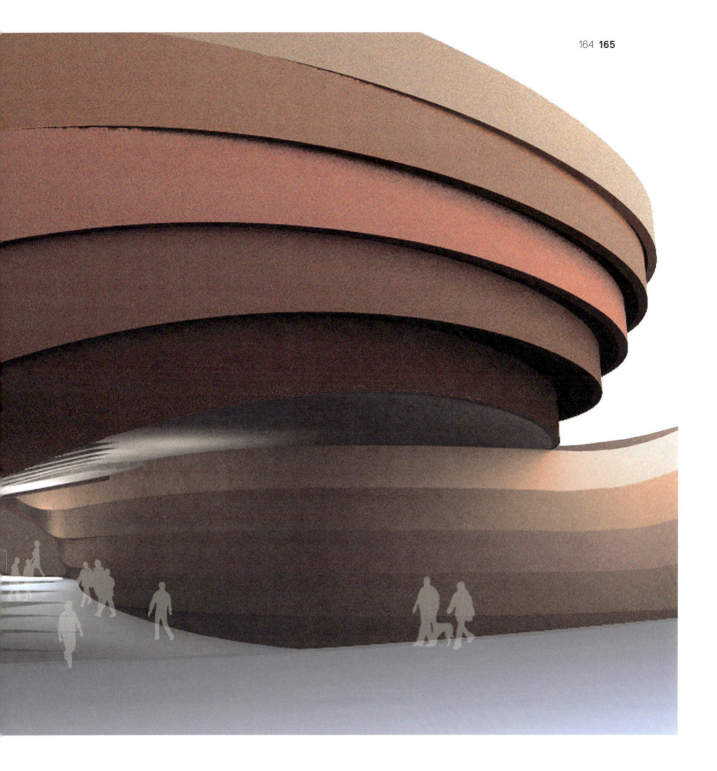

Notify Showroom, Milan. 2008 – ongoing
Interior design and centerpiece sculpture

Ohayon Villa, Marrakesh. 2007–ongoing

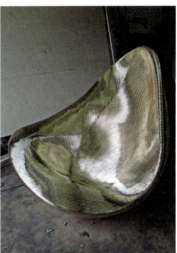

<Southern Hemisphere   Thumbprint>

In recent years Arad has renewed his passion for the expressiveness of steel and bronze in collaborations with such diverse producers as Mourmans, the renowned Italian metal-handicraft production company Marzorati-Ronchetti, and small craftsmen all over Europe. The outcome has been a series of sculptural pieces that are a pretext for Arad to test ideas about balance, smoothness, reflection, and patina, as well as to display his virtuoso technical and aesthetic prowess. Southern Hemisphere has been made in bronze and patinated superplastic aluminum, while Thumbprint is formed with polished stainless steel rods painstakingly applied by hand.

Southern Hemisphere. 2007 [opposite]
Patinated superplastic aluminum
51×52×52" (129.5×132.1×132.1 cm)
Edition by The Gallery Mourmans, The Netherlands
Southern Hemisphere. 2007 [top left]
Polished superplastic aluminum
53½×52⁵⁄₁₆×54⁵⁄₁₆" (136×133×138 cm)
Edition by The Gallery Mourmans, The Netherlands

Sketch for Southern Hemisphere (2007). N.d. [top right]
Thumbprint. 2007 [bottom left & right]
Polished stainless steel rod
65×59×60" (165.1×149.9×152.4 cm)
Edition by Ron Arad Associates, London

Afterthought

While making Southern Hemisphere (pages 168–69),
Arad found his eye and imagination caught by two
formed, untrimmed plates sitting in the workshop.
He decided to treat these slabs as if they were an
otherworldly and powerful press, locking a volume
between them so that it seemed to be compressed—
and called this idea an "afterthought." The red version
dramatizes the effect, highlighting the landscape
within the piece.

Afterthought. 2007 [left]
Bronze-patinated superplastic aluminum
6' 1½" × 7' × 62" (186.7 × 213.4 × 157.5 cm)
Edition by The Gallery Mourmans, The Netherlands
Afterthought. 2007 [right]
Polished and color-polished superplastic aluminum
45⅝ × 68⅛ × 60⅝" (116 × 173 × 154 cm)
Edition by The Gallery Mourmans, The Netherlands

Afterthought. 2007 [opposite]
Polished superplastic aluminum
67 × 67¾ × 67¾" (170 × 172 × 172 cm)
Edition by The Gallery Mourmans, The Netherlands

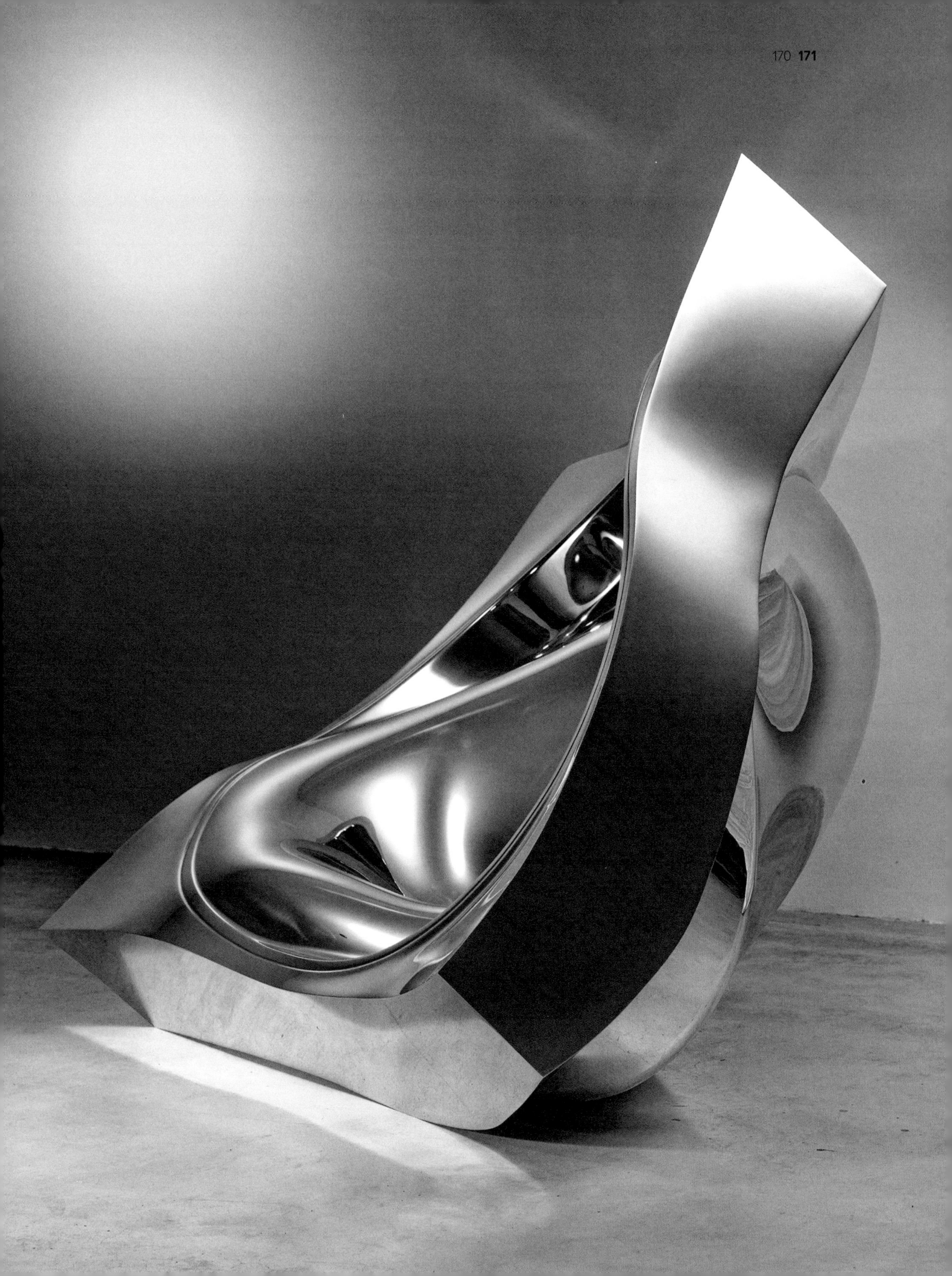

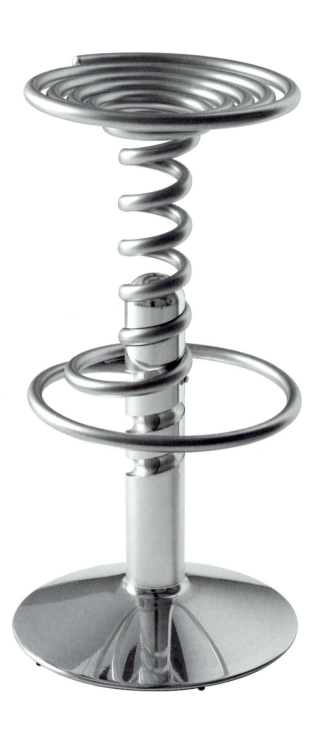

Screw. 2006 [left]
Aluminum and stainless steel
H. 33⁷⁄₁₆" (85 cm), top diam. 15¾" (40 cm), base diam. 23⅝" (60 cm)
Manufactured by Driade SpA, Italy
Sketch for Screw (2006). N.d. [right]

Y's Store>

One of Arad's most prominent commercial-architecture projects was the flagship store for Y's, the Tokyo-based clothing company established, in 1972, by fashion designer Yohji Yamamoto. The store, now dismantled, was located in Tokyo in Roppongi Hills, the well-known commercial development that opened in 2003. Arad's dynamic scheme featured four large turntables built into the floor, each topped by a floor-to-ceiling sculptural column made of thirty-four tubular loops of aluminum. During business hours, the turntables rotated extremely slowly—subtly enough to go unnoticed by the customers. Visitors entered and exited through a revolving door, symbolically echoing the turntables' movement. At night the turntables sped up, giving the empty store an unusual after-hours energy, visible through the windows. The four columns resembled huge Slinky coils, and each one of their rings could be pulled out to provide hanging racks for clothes. Arad's consideration of details extended down to the hangers, which had knob handles to make them easy to lift from the racks. The design also included a large, epoxy-coated red steel counter.

∧Ha-Yarkon

Located on Ha-Yarkon Street, on Tel Aviv's waterfront, this luxury apartment building's staggered-floor design is meant to maximize each unit's view of the ocean.

Apartment on Ha-Yarkon Street, Tel Aviv. 2006 – ongoing [above]

Y's Store, Roppongi Hills, Tokyo. 2003 [following pages]

Ringoletto. 2007 [left]
Platinum plated on porcelain
Three vases: h. 6¼" (16 cm), 7½" (19 cm), and 9⁷⁄₁₆" (24 cm)
Manufactured by Rosenthal AG, Germany
Sketch for Ringoletto (2007). N.d. [right]

Squashed Vipps. 2008
Polished stainless steel
Extended: h. 17¾" (45 cm), diam. 13¾" (35 cm);
squashed: h. 13¾" (35 cm), diam. 13¾" (35 cm)
Manufactured by Vipp, Denmark, altered by Ron Arad

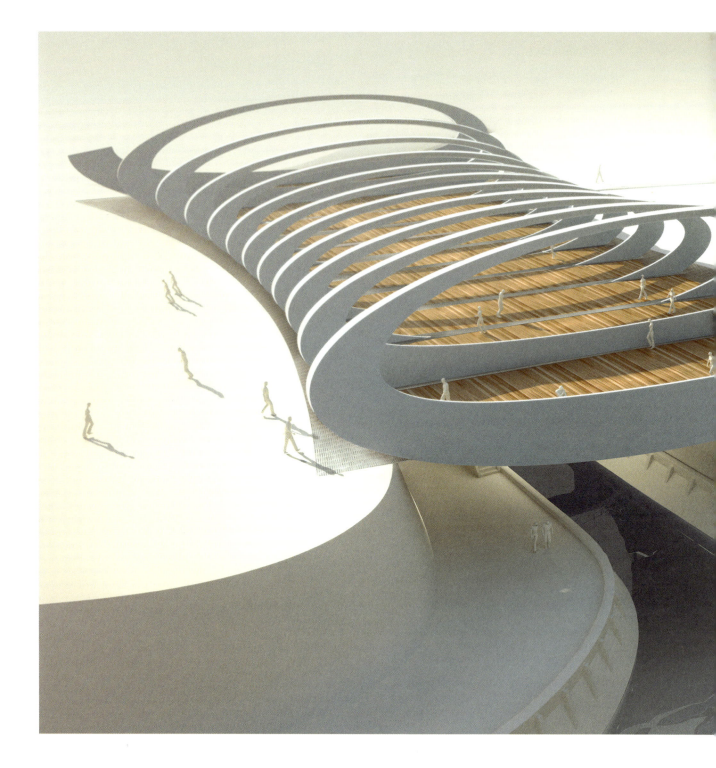

Olympic Bridge, London. Project. 2007
Design for main pedestrian bridge in the Olympic Village
for the 2012 Olympic Games

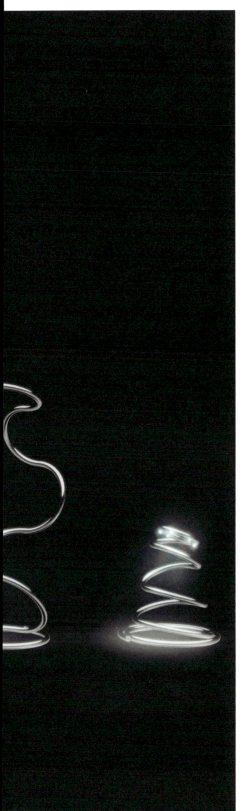

PizzaKobra

This lamp, which transforms itself from a coil as flat as a pizza to a sinuous, rising metal cobra with a single glowing red eye (its on/off switch), is as surprising as it is playful, as much like a twisty Tangle Toy as a very efficient and flexible light source. With its tubular-aluminum sections — except for the base, which is heavier steel, for balance — and six LEDs that can be oriented in any direction, the PizzaKobra can be adjusted to suit any lighting requirements.

PizzaKobra. 2007
Chromed steel, aluminum, and LEDs
Extended: h. 28⅞" (73.3 cm), diam. 10¼" (26 cm);
collapsed: h.¾" (1.9 cm), diam.10¼" (26 cm)
Manufactured by iGuzzini illuminazione SpA, Italy

Notify Bag>

For the Notify Bag, which was commissioned by the denim-clothing manufacturer Notify, Arad was inspired by the unique quality of a liquid-crystal film, often bonded to windows, that goes from transparent to opaque — public to private — at the touch of a switch. The leather bag, designed like a coil that can expand to accommodate what it carries, has a window powered by a small battery, allowing its contents to be visible, or not.

Unidentified Fragrance Object. 2008 [above]
Zamac (zinc, aluminum, magnesium, and copper) alloy
4¾×2¾" (12×7 cm)
Manufactured by Métapack, Pinard, and Valois for Kenzo Parfums

Notify Bag. Prototype. 2008 [opposite]
Leather and polycarbonate
25⁹⁄₁₆×15⁹⁄₁₆" (65×39.5 cm)
Prototype by Notify, France

Not Made by Hand, Not Made in China

Not Made by Hand, Not Made in China is a series of limited-edition objects — vases, sculptures, lamps, and bowls — that Arad presented at the Galleria Gió Marconi in April 2000, on the occasion of the annual furniture fair in Milan. The series is unified by its manner of production: all of the objects were made by a rapid-prototyping technique (also called 3D printing), which at that time was commonly used to create one-off models that would later be produced in series using traditional manufacturing processes. In rapid prototyping, computer-controlled lasers read instructions from computer-generated design files and translate them into a physical object through stereo-lithography (the selective curing of resin) or laser sintering (the fusing of grains of polyamide powder); Arad treated the results of this process as final products rather than templates, turning rapid prototyping into an advanced production method and eliminating the difference between prototype and serial product. Arad thinks of these objects as grown from the bottom up, in contrast to the top-down processes by which objects are generally made: molded, formed, or assembled. The vases, rendered in white resin by selective laser sintering, are guaranteed to be unique, as the digital design files from which they were created have been destroyed. The Coupe Banana Bowl is formed from a sample of Arad's handwriting (reading "Not Made by Hand"), extruded in a concave form. The Ge-Off Sphere, a coiled ceiling lamp that expands and contracts, was first executed in epoxy resin before the final edition of twenty was made in polyamide. The title of the series is exquisitely connected to a particular moment in the history of design and in Arad's career: he was grappling with a surprising number of cheap knockoffs of his work manufactured in China as well as with the promise of these new rapid-prototyping techniques.

Coupe Banana Bowl. 2000 [top]
Epoxy resin
39³⁄₈ × 15³⁄₄ × 7⁷⁄₈" (100 × 40 × 20 cm)
Edition by The Gallery Mourmans, The Netherlands
The Original File Was Destroyed On... 1999 [bottom]
Epoxy resin and laser-sintered polyamide
H. 19⁵⁄₈" (50 cm), diam. 11¹³⁄₁₆" (30 cm)
Edition by Ron Arad Associates, London

Ge-Off Sphere. 2000 [opposite]
Laser-sintered polyamide
H. variable, diam. 19⁵⁄₈" (50 cm)
Edition by The Gallery Mourmans, The Netherlands

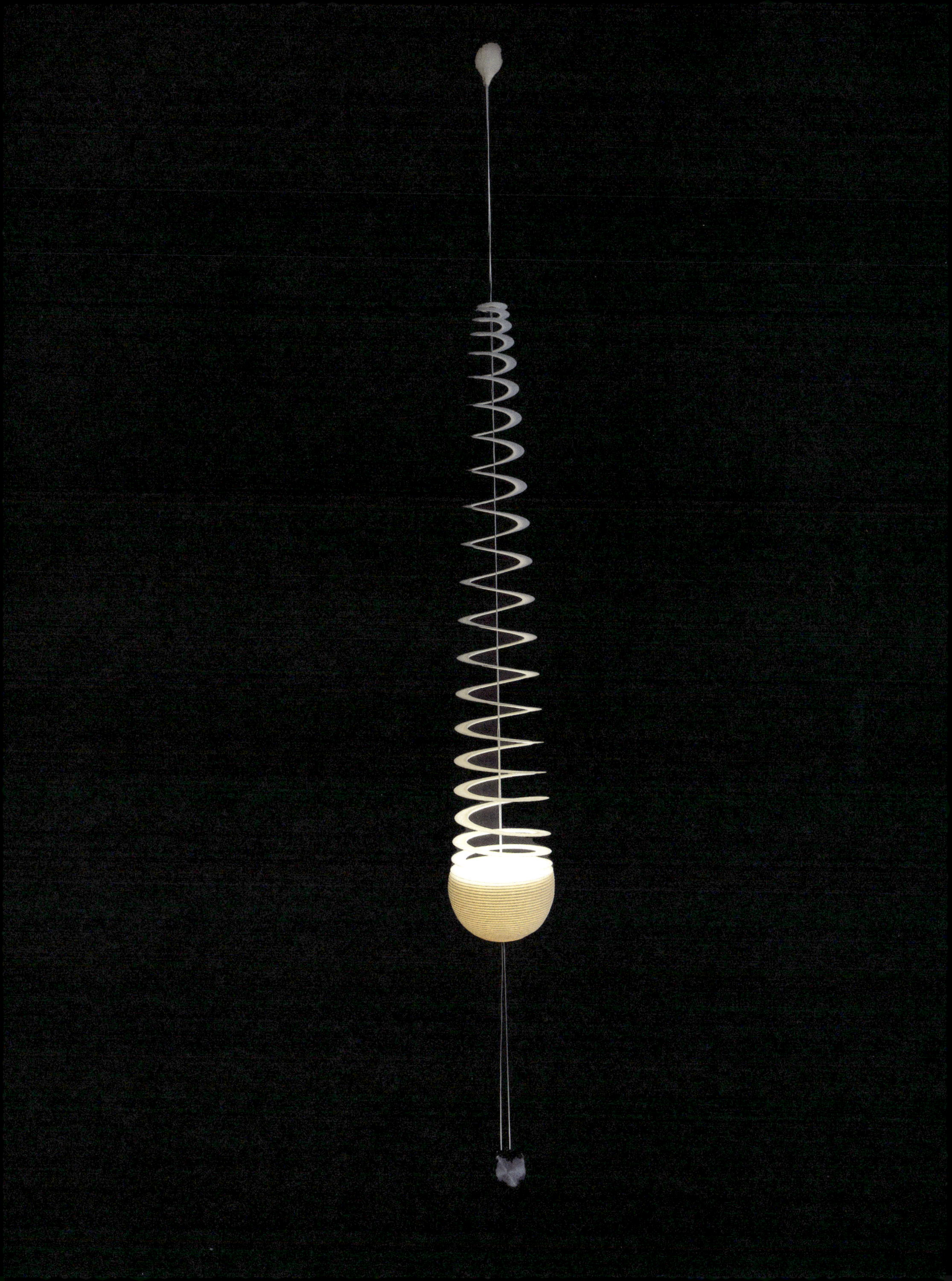

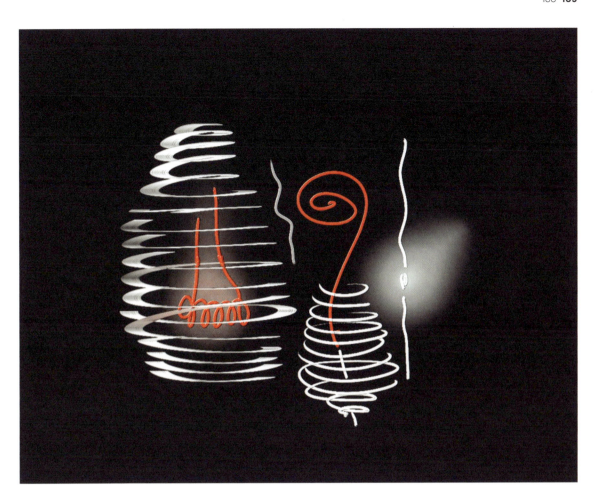

Ge-Off Sphere. 2000 [opposite]
Laser-sintered polyamide
H. variable, diam. 19⅝" (50 cm)
Edition by The Gallery Mourmans, The Netherlands
Sketch for Ge-Off Sphere (2000). N.d. [above]

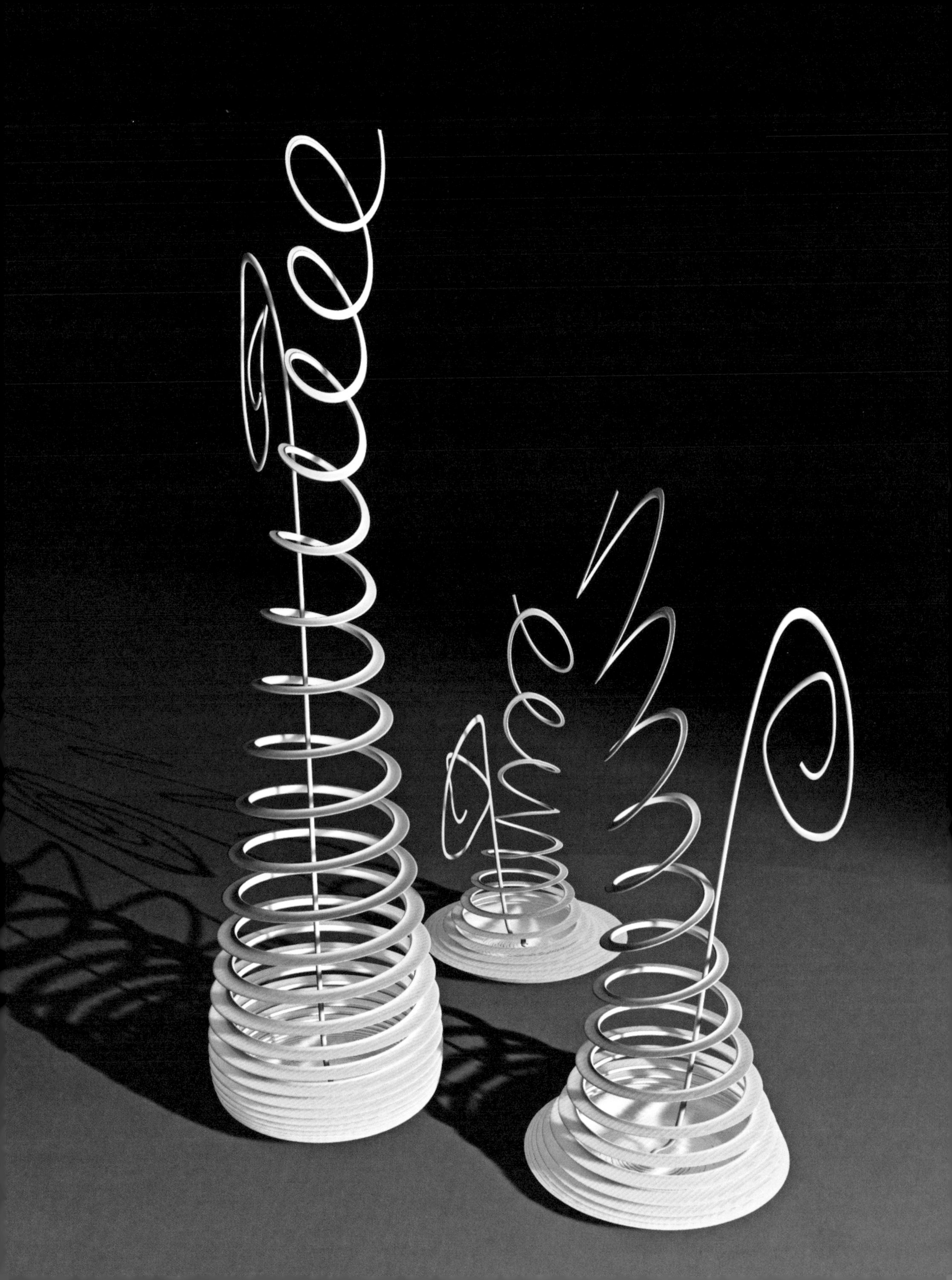

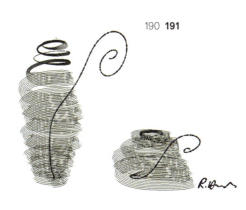

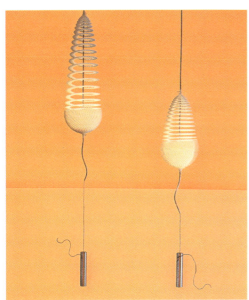

<Bouncing Vases

Part of the Not Made by Hand, Not Made in China series, these vases and lamps are made using rapid-prototyping technology. The edition was produced by The Gallery Mourmans, and the lamps are named after the lighting designer Ingo Maurer, one of Arad's closest friends, and Yuki Tango, the head of Arad's design team in the early 2000s. In these bouncing pieces, always shown with an accompanying video, Arad exploits rapid manufacturing's potential to micro-manage both the form and the behavior of the resin it employs.

Bouncing Vases. 2001 [opposite & top left]
Laser-sintered polyamide
Each 10 5/8 × 3 15/16 × 6 5/16" (27 × 10 × 16 cm)
Edition by The Gallery Mourmans, The Netherlands
Sketch for Bouncing Vases (2001). N.d. [top right]

Hot Ingo. 2001 [bottom left]
Laser-sintered polyamide, stainless steel, and xelogen bulb
6' 2 7/16" × 7 1/16" × 7 1/16" (189 × 18 × 18 cm)
Edition by The Gallery Mourmans, The Netherlands
Hot Tango. 2001 [bottom right]
Laser-sintered polyamide, stainless steel, and LEDs
48 7/16" × 8 7/8" × 8 7/8" (123 × 22.5 × 22.5 cm)
Edition by The Gallery Mourmans, The Netherlands

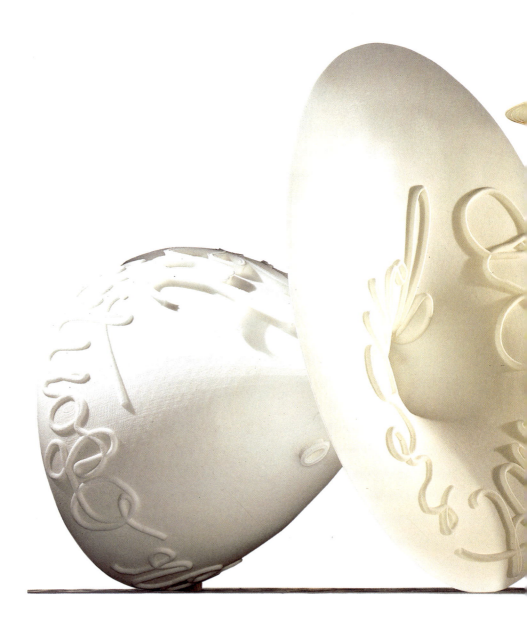

Perfect Vases

The Perfect Vases, another set of objects produced using rapid prototyping, are inscribed with handwriting that reads, "virtuoso reality," "perfect," and "do not recycle."

Perfect Vases. 2001
Laser-sintered polyamide and epoxy resin
Two vases: each h. 10⅝" (27 cm), diam. 16⁹⁄₁₆" (42 cm)
Edition by The Gallery Mourmans, The Netherlands

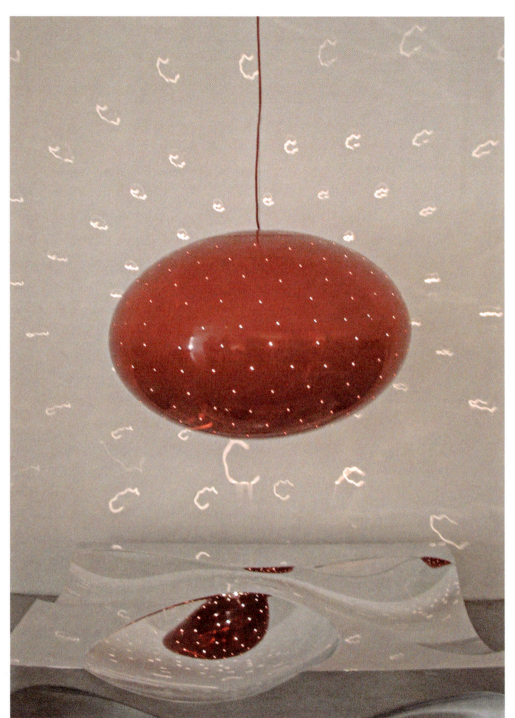

I.P.C.O. (Inverted Pinhole Camera Obscura). 2001
Fiberglass, polyester, and incandescent light bulb
Diam. 39⅜" (100 cm)
Edition by The Gallery Mourmans, The Netherlands

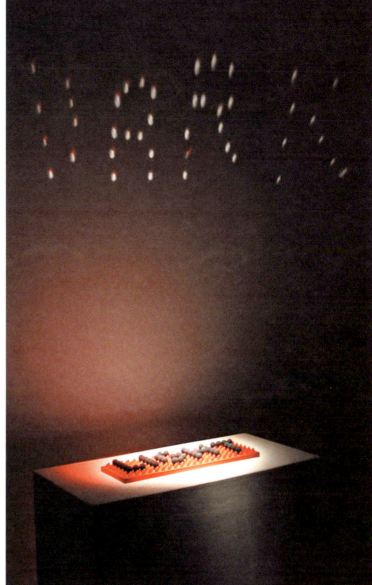

<I.P.C.O.

I.P.C.O. (Inverted Pinhole Camera Obscura) appears to be a simple hanging lamp but is in reality a reversed pinhole camera, which allows an image to be projected from inside its fiberglass body out onto the walls of a darkened room. Arad first experimented with "writing" various words by modifying a standard incandescent bulb's filament, and then settled for a somewhat abstract image of the filament itself. I.P.C.O. was produced by The Gallery Mourmans, in an edition of fifty, and was first presented at the Milan Furniture Fair, in 2001, as part of *Delight in Dedark,* a show at the Galleria Gió Marconi.

Ballpark>

Ballpark, a prototype developed by Arad for Ingo Maurer's lighting company, consists of a tray holding a group of small rubber balls, each with a slice cut out of it and replaced with a mirror. Each ball, oriented to catch the light, reflects a single pixel onto a wall, spelling out words or images; because there are so many possible angles and each ball can be independently manipulated, the text on the wall can be different from—even the opposite of—what is shown on the tray. Ballpark was presented at the Milan Furniture Fair in 2001, in *Delight in Dedark,* which also featured Arad's curtain of the same name (pages 196–97) and I.P.C.O.

Ballpark. Prototype. 2001
Silicone, steel, and rubber
3 ¹⁵⁄₁₆ × 19 ¹¹⁄₁₆ × 11 ¹³⁄₁₆" (10 × 50 × 30 cm)
Prototype by Ron Arad Associates, London

Delight in Dedark

The exhibition *Delight in Dedark,* at the 2001 Milan
Furniture Fair, featured—along with Ballpark and
I.P.C.O. (pages 194–95)—one of Arad's most spectacular works: a curtain made of silicone rods onto which
moving images were projected. Visitors could walk
through the curtain, also named Delight in Dedark, and
feel as if they were inside the images; sensors placed
near the installation translated visitors' movements into
a visible reaction in the image, turning the curtain
into a vertical pool of rippling liquid.

Delight in Dedark. 2001
Silicone, steel, and rubber
11' 5¹³⁄₁₆" × 22' 11⁹⁄₁₆" × ¹³⁄₁₆" (350×700×2 cm)
Edition by The Gallery Mourmans, The Netherlands

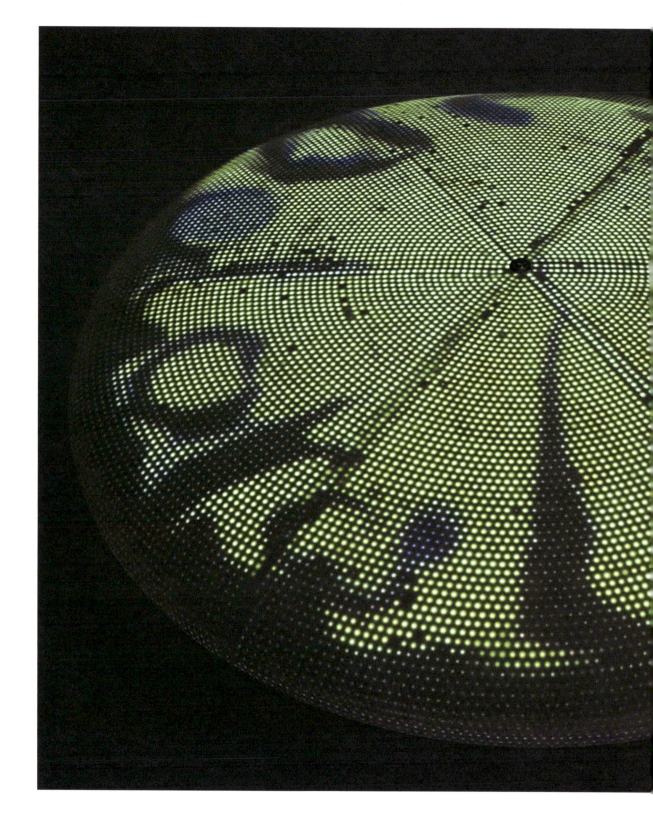

Lo-Rez-Dolores-Tabula-Rasa. 2004
Corian, fiber-optics, projector, and DVD
H. 13½" (34.3 cm), diam. 66" (167.6 cm)
Edition by The Gallery Mourmans, The Netherlands

Lo-Rez-Dolores-Tabula-Rasa

Lo-Rez-Dolores-Tabula-Rasa, a lens-shaped table, was part of an exhibition of the same name at the Galleria Gió Marconi, in Milan. The design was one result of Arad's experimental work with Corian, a material that has been around for forty years but is not widely used in sophisticated domestic design applications beyond kitchen counters. To remedy this, its manufacturer, the chemical company DuPont, approached Arad about finding new, experimental, and innovative applications for it. Arad decided to use a very thin sheet of Corian as a rear-projection screen, which he combined with twenty-two thousand fiber-optic pixels, to animate the tabletop with images and film that appear, as the name indicates, in low reso-lution. When not in use as a screen, the table is smooth and white — a beautiful blank slate, or tabula rasa, that forms a vivid contrast to the common LED screen, which Arad has described as a black hole.

Sketch for Lo-Rez-Dolores-Tabula-Rasa (2004). N.d.

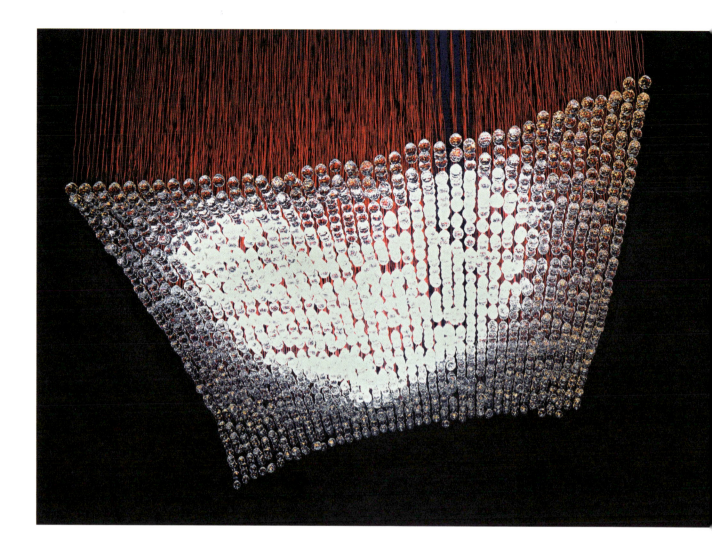

^Miss Haze

A year after Lolita (following page), Arad designed his second lighting fixture for Crystal Palace. Miss Haze is a combination chandelier/writing board consisting of 2,500 clear crystals, each equipped with an LED and hanging from an electrical wire. The crystals, functioning like pixels, display text or images sent from a handheld PDA via Bluetooth wireless connection.

Miss Haze. 2005 [above & opposite]
Crystals, LEDs, electronics, and remote drawing tablet
Dimensions unknown
Edition by Swarovski, Austria

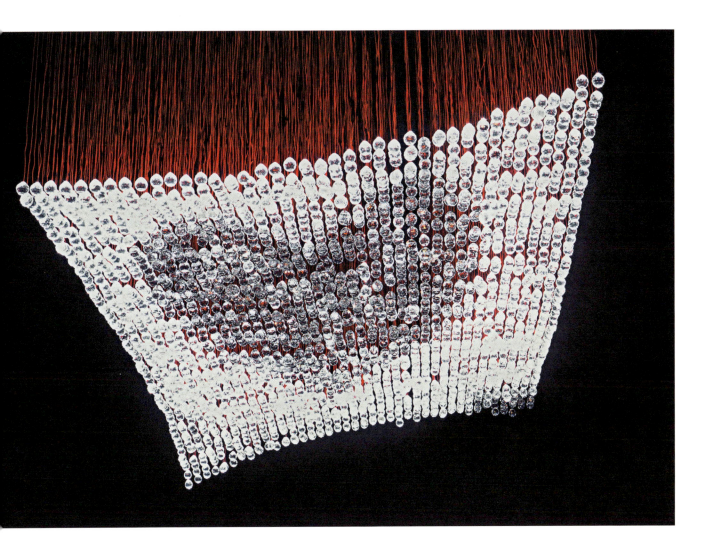

Lolita>

When Nadja Swarovski set out to build a new division for her family's company, Swarovski Crystal, she invited Arad to reinvent the chandelier as a juxtaposition of traditional form with modern technology. The new collection of chandeliers, called Crystal Palace, launched in 2002, and Arad's Lolita was ready in 2004. Made with 2,100 crystals and 1,050 white LEDs, Lolita takes the shape of a flat ribbon wound into a corkscrew shape. The ribbon contains 31 processors that enable the display of SMS text messages sent to Lolita's mobile phone number; these messages appear at the top of the chandelier and wind down the ribbon's curves,

slowly enough to give bystanders time to read, creating the impression that the chandelier is spinning ever so slightly. The name is the result of grace under pressure: on the phone with Swarovski and pressed for a name, Arad thought of another work in progress, his LED-riddled Lo-Rez-Dolores-Tabula-Rasa (pages 198–99), and from there went to "Lolita"—the nickname of Vladimir Nabokov's Dolores Haze. The name stuck, creating not only a saucy entry in many a design buff's phone book but a further literary association as well: as a journalist pointed out to Arad, Nabokov's novel begins, "Lolita, light of my life…"

Lolita. 2004 [following page, left]
Crystals and LEDs
H. 59" (150 cm), top-plate diam. 43¼" (110 cm)
Edition by Swarovski, Austria
Sketch for Lolita (2004). N.d. [following page, right]

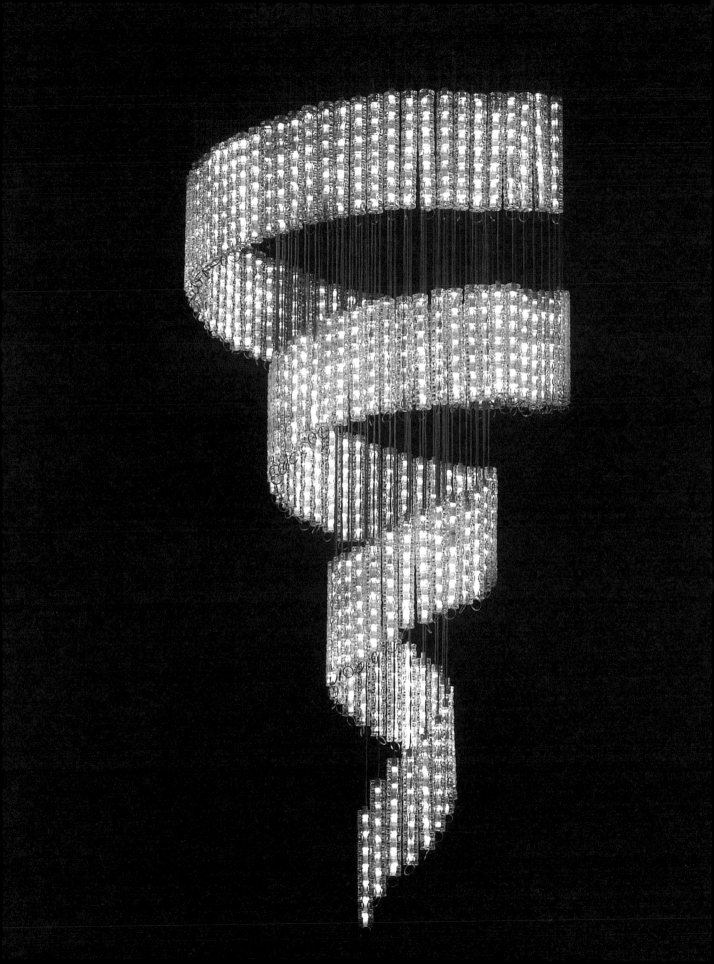

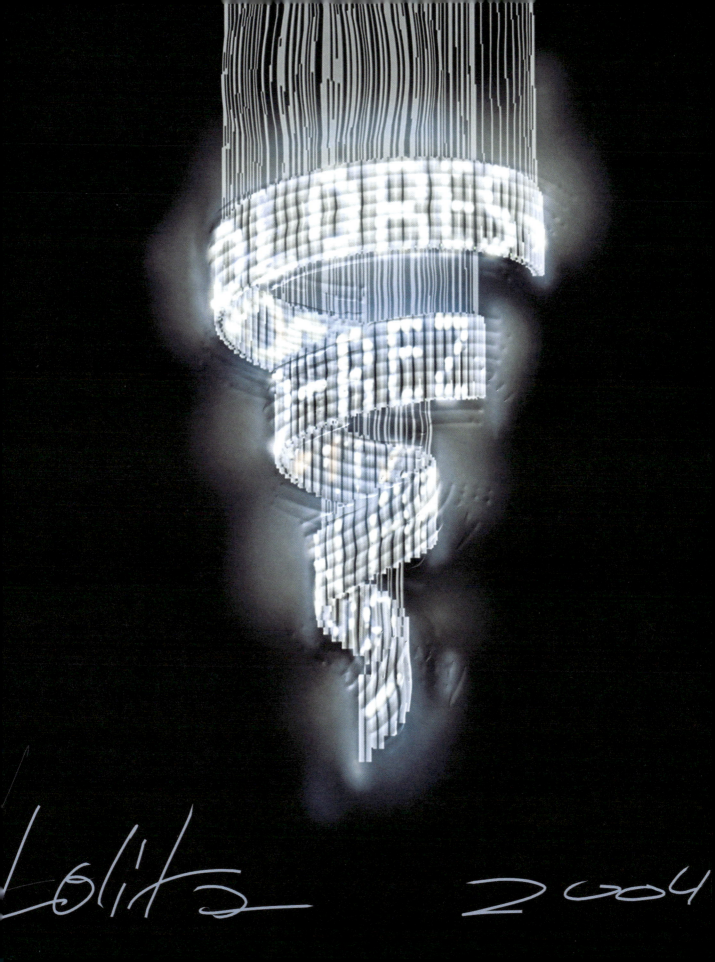

Lolita 2004

YOU LOOK UP ESCAPE ARTIST

JONATHAN SAFRAN FOER

Like most good things, my love for dictionary illustrations began accidentally. As a child I simply wanted to find images, in my parents' staid library, of BOOBS, ASS, VAGINA, and the like. I never found them. But I didn't stop playing the game. The game changed.

It's fun to try to decipher the weird logic of dictionary illustrations. Why is there an image of a guitar's neck (and not a carved balustrade or anguished Jew) with the definition for FRET? Why a drawing, and not a photo, of COLTRANE, JOHN? And why, for that matter, are there ten illustrations for NAIL and not one for SCREW? (SCREW being one of the first words I looked up.) The reasoning isn't obvious, and seems not to take into account how important or familiar a word is, or how easy to illustrate it might be. WEST INDIAN MANATEE has an illustration, WHEEL does not.

There are things—pornography, the taste of water—that are impossible to define but easy to recognize. Ron Arad's genius is such a thing. Is he a designer? (Industrial? Furniture?) A sculptor? An architect? A conceptual artist? Should it matter? And if not, should it matter that it shouldn't matter?

The problem with pinning Arad down is not that he doesn't fit any of the potential descriptions, but that he can't be contained by them. Imagine looking up CORKSCREW and finding an image of a Swiss Army Knife. Imagine looking up DESIGNER and finding Arad.

Not long after our accidental first meeting, I had the good fortune of spending two days at Arad's studio on Chalk Farm Road. He'd picked me up at the train station in a bizarre Japanese vehicle that would fit no one's mental image of a CAR. He was wearing a felt contraption on his head—something sort of like a HAT. On his feet were, if I'm not mistaken, SHOES, but not like any I'd ever seen.

And STUDIO isn't quite the right word for where Ron works, as it's also a museum, and, itself, a sculpture. Among the things I saw that day: the design for a restaurant that swings, on a pivot, atop a mountain peak; a handbag that, by moving the clips of the shoulder strap, could transform itself into three other kinds of bags; the interior of an opera house; a stainless steel ping-pong table, ingeniously angled in toward the net to slow the game down; a rolling bookshelf; plans for a massive, levitating, reflective sphere; the radical redesign of the most important square in Jerusalem; a better stool; a hotel lobby that bunches like cloth... What do you call someone who makes all of these things?

It shouldn't matter that Arad can't be defined, but it matters that it shouldn't matter, because we live in a world in which it's embarrassing and worse not to have a quick answer to the question "What do you do?" We live in a world that loves dictionary illustrations for all the wrong reasons. Specialization is, in and of itself, valued; Google search results are regarded as wisdom; automated customer service asks you to choose which of the following three options describes your problem; museums have design departments, and sculpture and architecture departments. Arad was not made for this world.

Great artists are never made for the world in which they live. This is a definitional truth. Any artist who can, in his time, be classified, is necessarily a failure. (Of course Cézanne was a PAINTER, Brancusi a SCULPTOR, and Prouvé a DESIGNER, but each did what he did for the first time. Until they were adored, and sometimes even while they were adored, they were sources of confusion and frustration.) Classification is another way of saying we already know what you are. Art requires unfamiliarity.

Nietzsche—who wasn't exactly a philosopher, writer, or theorist—wrote that everything we have a word for is already dead to us. The problem with words is that they are bad approximations and self-fulfilling prophecies. Words give life, and words kill.

I once read an essay by a linguist about the continued creation of Modern Hebrew. Until the mid-1970s, he wrote, there wasn't a word for frustrated. And so until the mid-'70s, no Hebrew speaker experienced frustration. Should his wife turn to him in the car and ask why he'd fallen so conspicuously quiet, he would search his incomplete dictionary of emotions and say, "I'm UPSET." Or, "I'm ANNOYED." Or, "I'm IRRITATED." This might have been, itself, merely frustrating, were it not for the problem that we become what we say we are. The man in the car says he is upset, annoyed, or irritated and becomes upset, annoyed, or irritated. Once the word entered the language, the FRUSTRATION of millions of Israelis was suddenly given life.

Or was emotion killed? Because they weren't really FRUSTRATED, were they?

They were what they were, which was different for each, and different each time. FRUSTRATION was simply a closer approximation than UPSET, ANNOYED, or IRRITATED. And so Israelis were able to feel something closer to what they actually felt. Is there something more to aspire to?

"There are only two kinds of people," Oscar Wilde wrote, "the charming and the tedious." The same could be said of objects. When we encounter a chair, there are many questions that we can't help but ask about it. Is it STABLE? Is it COMFORTABLE? Is it ATTRACTIVE? Is it NEW? And so on. And then it either stays with us or it doesn't. Those are the only two ways it can go.

It is our inability to name them that makes certain things stay with us.

Everything we have a word for is already dead to us, and those things we can't pin down stay alive. Arad's chairs are WEIRD, and BEAUTIFUL, and ARRESTING, and MONUMENTAL, and INTIMATE, and FUNNY, and somehow DEEP. But that's not why they stay with us. They stay with us because they aren't really chairs. Or sculptures. Or pieces of architecture. They are what they are, not concessions to a form, and not approximations of something else.

Turn this page sideways and see how words about art are like the bars of a prison. Arad is an escape artist, constantly finding ways to squeeze through the definitions. There is nothing more for an artist to aspire to than such elusiveness.

Like most good things, my friendship with Arad began accidentally. We were sitting across from each other at a dinner in a city that neither of us called home. It was a celebration that neither of us was exactly privy to. After a few minutes of silently picking at salads, he asked me what I did. I told him I was a WRITER, and felt that familiar disappointment of being something.

A WRITER of what?

Of NOVELS.

What NOVELS?

I told him. He had been reading my second book on the flight over. It's possible that it was the chance of that encounter that has sustained our friendship for this long.

I asked him what he did.

He laughed.

He wasn't avoiding my question.

May 2008
Brooklyn, New York

LENDERS TO THE EXHIBITION

Stedelijk Museum, Amsterdam
The Museum of Fine Arts, Houston
Collection Boisbuchet Workshops, Lessac, France
The Museum of Modern Art, New York
Centre Pompidou, Musée national d'art moderne/Centre de création industrielle, Paris
Vitra Design Museum, Weil am Rhein, Germany

Andrea Aranow, New York
Collection Sergio Casoli, Rome, Italy
Jean and Annie Galvani. Private collection, France
Collection Michael G. Jesselson, New York
Collection Reed and Delphine Krakoff
Christiane Leister, Switzerland
Collection Aby J. Rosen
Collection Jérôme and Emmanuelle de Noirmont, Paris
Collection Ron and Ann Pizzuti
M.J.S. Collection, Paris
Jerome L. and Ellen Stern

Anonymous lenders

Ben Brown Fine Arts
François Laffanour, Galerie Downtown, Paris
The Scorpio Collection, courtesy of Phillips de Pury & Company

Museo Alessi
ddc domus design collection
Driade
iGuzzini illuminazione
Kartell
Magis
The Miyake Issey Foundation
Moroso SpA, Udine, Italy
Notify
Vitra

ACKNOWLEDGMENTS

Ron Arad: No Discipline was a project unique in complexity and scope. During the planning of this ambitious exhibition and this catalogue we relied on the generosity and exceptional professionalism of a large group of colleagues, lenders, and consultants to whom we will be forever indebted. This space is too short to thank them all, and too short to mention all the wonderful MoMA colleagues who have made it happen.

We wish to thank Glenn D. Lowry, Director of The Museum of Modern Art, and the Museum's Trustees, in particular Ronald S. Lauder, Honorary Chairman, for their unwavering support of this project. We also thank the exhibition's funders, Notify and The Contemporary Arts Council of The Museum of Modern Art.

We're deeply grateful for the generosity of the lenders, whom we thank on behalf of Ron Arad and our colleagues at the other two host museums, for agreeing to part temporarily with their works. Their names—or at least some of their names—appear on the previous page; here we would like to thank two gallerists who facilitated some important loans, Marc Benda and Ernest Mourmans, and their collaborators Nicole Schechter, Rachel Compton, and Elita Janssen.

Several institutions generously agreed to lend us objects, and we would like to thank them: at the Musée national d'art moderne, Centre Georges Pompidou, Paris, Director Alfred Pacquement, along with Martine Silie, Ludivine Rousseaux, Marielle Dagault, Martine Moinot, and Marine Sentenac; at the Stedelijk Museum, Amsterdam, Director Gijs van Tuyl and Ankie van den Berg, Anniek Vrij, and Maria Hendriks; at The Museum of Fine Arts, Houston, Director Peter Marzio, Cindi Strauss, and Erika Franck; and at the Vitra Design Museum, Weil am Rhein, Germany, Director Alexander von Vegesack, Serge Mauduit, Richard Adler, and Boguslaw Ubik-Perski.

Together with Patricia Juncosa-Vecchierini, my indomitable curatorial partner for so many exhibitions, I would like to thank the leaders of all the different MoMA departments involved in the installation, first and foremost Jennifer Russell, and then Ramona Bannayan, Maria DeMarco Beardsley, Jim Coddington, and Rob Jung and Sarah Wood.

In the Department of Architecture and Design, we are deeply grateful to Barry Bergdoll and to the entire staff, especially Curatorial Assistants Aidan O'Connor—who also participated in the installation as part of the curatorial team—and Margot Weller. Special mention goes to Emma Presler, Department Manager, and Shayna Gentiluomo, Administrative Assistant. Several brilliant interns worked on this project: Lesley Merz, Stephanie Johnson, Edgar Almaguer, and Hunter Palmer.

The installation, designed by Ron Arad Associates and built by Marzorati Ronchetti in Italy, was incomparably overseen and produced in New York by Betty Fisher; the exhibition was funded, coordinated, realized, publicized, promoted, and installed by a great team that included, in alphabetical order and across departments, Nancy Adelson, Nicholas Apps, Laura Beiles, Todd Bishop, Sara Bodinson, Brigitta Bungard, Allegra Burnette, Claire Corey, Shannon Darrough, Margo Delidow, Margaret Doyle, Mike Gibbons, Roger Griffith, Mary Hannah, August Heffner, Pablo Helguera, Julia Hoffman, Charlie Kalinowski, Tom Krueger, Henry Lanman, Bic Leu, Jennifer Manno, K Mita, Kim Mitchell, Susan Palamara, Lauren Stakias, Daniela Stigh, Rebecca Stokes, Jennifer Tobias, Wendy Woon, Paola Zanzo-Sahl, and many others.

The Department of Publications led by Christopher Hudson with lieutenants Kara Kirk, David Frankel, and Marc Sapir, gets the kudos for this complex and wonderful book, edited by Emily Hall, produced by Christina Grillo, and designed by Hjalti Karlsson, Jan Wilker, and Nicole Jacek of karlssonwilker. We also wish to thank The International Council of The Museum of Modern Art, and in particular President Jo Carole Lauder, for funding this publication. For their quotes, interviews, and commentary we thank Nina Stritzler-Levine; Christopher Frayling, Rector of the Royal College of Art from 1996 to 2009; Anthony Dunne; and many tutors and students from the RCA's Design Products program.

For their contribution to this book and for their partnership in the organization of the show, I would like to thank my colleagues Marie-Laure Jousset at the Centre Pompidou and Ingeborg de Roode at the Stedelijk Museum.

The exhibition installation wouldn't have been possible without the generosity of Yves Bouvier, lender of Arad's *Cage sans frontières*, the structure that displayed all the works; Michael Maharam and the Maharam company, which donated the fabric that wraps the structure, also deserves a particular mention, as does the OKE Group, which created the fixtures that anchored it. We also would like to thank Bill Costa, Keith Domescik, and Roberto Travaglia.

Dulcis in fundo, this project could never have happened without the extraordinary people who work with Ron Arad, from his partner Caroline Thorman, who has spearheaded the studio since its very beginning and who offered us all of her deep knowledge and experience, to Michael Castellana, who managed the installation's design and production, and Clodagh Latimer and the whole Ron Arad Associates office. And the project would never have happened without Ron Arad himself—without his curiosity and daring, without his talent and open-mindedness, and without his deep commitment to art and design.

Paola Antonelli
Senior Curator, Department of Architecture and Design

SELECTED BIBLIOGRAPHY

Albus, Volker. *Design Classics: The Bookworm by Ron Arad.* Trans. Annette Wiethüchter. Frankfurt am Main: Verlag Form, 1997.

Albus, Volker, and Cedric Price, with an introduction by Ettore Sottsass. *Ron Arad Associates: One Off Three.* London: Artemis Architectural Publishing, 1993.

Arad, Ron. "Inspiration: Ron Arad." *Interiors*, Spring–Summer 2008.

———. "These Things I Know." *The Observer.* September 26, 2004, http://www.guardian.co.uk/theobserver/2004/sep/26/artsfeatures.

Collings, Matthew. *Ron Arad Talks to Matthew Collings about Designing Chairs, Vases, Buildings and....* London: Phaidon, 2004.

Friedman, Barry, et al. *Ron Arad: A Retrospective Exhibition*, 1981–2004. New York: Barry Friedman, 2005.

Guidot, Raymond, and Olivier Boissière. *Ron Arad.* Paris: Dis Voir, 1998.

Haden-Guest, Anthony. "Ron Arad...." *Interview* 39, no. 4 (May 2009): 66–69, 110.

Hochman, Carol, and Sarah Natkins. *Ron Arad: Paved with Good Intentions: An Installation by Ron Arad.* New York: Friedman Benda; Maastricht, The Netherlands: The Gallery Mourmans, 2007.

Manson, Neil. "Chairmaster." Artnet Web site, http://www.artnet.com/magazine/reviews/manson/manson5-25-05.asp.

"Ron Arad." Web site of Design Museum, London, http://www.designmuseum.org/design/ron-arad.

"Ron Arad: No Discipline." Centre Pompidou Web site, http://www.centrepompidou.fr/education/ressources/ENS-ronarad-EN/ENS-ronarad-EN.html.

Ron Arad: The Dogs Barked. Zurich: de Pury & Luxembourg, 2007.

Rushton, Susie. "Chair Man." *The Independent*, September 22, 2007.

Sanson, Anna. "The Year of A Rad: Ron Arad." *DAMn*, no. 20 (January–February 2009): 13.

Sudjic, Deyan. *Ron Arad.* London: Laurence King, 1999.

———. *Ron Arad: Restless Furniture.* London: Fourth Estate, 1989.

von Vegesack, Alexander, ed. *Ron Arad.* Weil am Rhein, Germany: Vitra Design Museum, 1990.

CHRONOLOGICAL INDEX OF WORKS BY RON ARAD IN THIS PUBLICATION

ALPHABETICAL INDEX OF WORKS BY RON ARAD IN THIS PUBLICATION

PHOTOGRAPH CREDITS

Alessi, photo Riccardo Bianchi: 120 (bottom left, center right); photo Softroom: 65.

Gabrielle Ammann: 80 (top left).

Archives Ron Arad Associates, London: 17, 21 (center), 27 (top and bottom left), 41 (right), 42 (bottom left and right), 46 (bottom), 52 (bottom), 54 (bottom), 59 (all), 62 (right), 63, 81 (top), 82 (bottom), 83 (bottom left and right), 86 (bottom), 87 (bottom), 89 (top), 95, 96 (right), 100 (bottom right), 101 (bottom), 107 (bottom), 108 (bottom), 110 (center right and left), 114, 117 (bottom), 120 (top and bottom right), 121 (top and bottom left), 129 (top), 138 (bottom), 169 (top right), 172 (right), 178 (right), 189, 191 (top right), 199, 203, back cover.

Photo courtesy Ron Arad Associates, London: 12 (all), 15 (right), 19, 20 (all), 21 (left), 23 (top right), 48 (bottom left and right), 56 (bottom left), 60–61, 81 (bottom right), 82, 83 (bottom left and right), 86 (top left), 88, 106, 111 (bottom left), 129 (bottom), 134–36, 169 (bottom left and right), 186–188, 190, 191 (top left), 191 (bottom right), 194–98, 200–202; photo G. Dagon: 23 (bottom left), 84–85; photo Perry Hagopian: 99; photo Wilhelm Moser: 42 (top right), 53 (top right), 120 (top left); photo Nacasa & Partners: 174–77; photo Tom Vack: 46 (top), 80 (bottom), 81 (bottom left), 97 (top), 110 (top left and right, bottom), 112–13, 118 (top), 191 (bottom left), 182–83.

Rendering by Ron Arad Associates, London: 100 (top and bottom left), 101 (top), 126–28, 132–33, 137, 160–61, 164–67, 173, 180, 185 (all).

Assa Ashuach: 145 (top left).

Auger-Loizeau 2004: 145 (top right).

Marloes ten Bhömer: 145 (bottom left).

Collection Boisbuchet Workshops, Lessac, France: 57 (top right).

Anke Bornemann / Harald Seick, Gabrielle Ammann–Designer's Gallery: 55.

Courtesy Ben Brown Fine Arts: 179.

Collection Centre Pompidou, Paris, Dist. RMN, photo Jacques Faujour: 33; photo Georges Meguerditchian: 97 (bottom); photo Philippe Migeat: 51 (top left); photo Jean-Claude Planchet: 58, 62 (bottom), 92, 131.

Centre Pompidou, Paris, photo Georges Meguerditchian: 28, 56 (bottom left [Sit!]).

©Marie Clérin–galerieDOWNTOWNfrançois laffanour: 57 (bottom left), 139 (bottom right).

CNAC / MNAM / Dist. Réunion des Musées Nationaux / Art Resource, NY, photo Jean-Claude Planchet: 43 (top and bottom).

Photo Claudia Costa: 130.

Michael Cross and Julie Mathias: 148 (bottom left).

Designer's Gallery–Gabrielle Ammann: 32, 115.

Photo courtesy Driade, Italy: 83 (top), 86 (top left), 87 (top), 103 (bottom left and right), 119, 172 (left).

Andrea Ferrari for Swarovski Crystal Palace: 148 (bottom right).

Photo courtesy Fiam Italia, Italy: 122.

Fonds national d'art contemporain, ministère de la Culture et de la Communication, Paris, photo Bruno Scotti: 52 (top).

Friedman Benda, New York, and The Gallery Mourmans, Maastricht: 138–39.

Friedman Benda, New York, photo Erik and Petra Hesmerg: 124;

The Gallery Mourmans, Maastricht, photo Erik and Petra Hesmerg: front cover, 26, 30, 38 (right); 35–36, 42 (top left), 47 (top left), 48 (top left and right, center left and right), 50 (all), 51 (center right), 53 (top left), 54 (top), 79, 89 (right), 90–91, 93 (all), 102, 103 (top), 109 (top left and right, bottom right), 111 (bottom right), 116 (top), 117 (top), 168, 169 (top left), 170–71.

Photo Erik and Petra Hesmerg, Amsterdam / the Netherlands: 14 (center and right), 16 (left), 34 (top right and left).

Photo courtesy Iguzzini, Italy: 182–83.

Photo Thibault Jeanson: 121 (right).

Photo courtesy Kartell, Italy: 64, 82 (top), 94 (all).

Kenzo Parfums: 184.

Photo Howard Kingsnorth: 29.

Photo Hannes Koch / rAndom International: 148 (center).

Onkar Kular: 156 (top right).

Photo courtesy Magis, Italy: 118 (bottom).

Peter Marigold: 145 (bottom right).

Photo Jean-Claude Meauxsoone: 78 (left).

Graeme Montgomery / TrunkArchive.com: 24.

Photo courtesy Moroso, Italy: 49, 96 (left), 104–5, 107 (top), 108 (top), 109 (bottom left), 138 (top), 162.

The Mugrabi Collection: 123 (top).

The Museum of Modern Art, New York, Imaging Services, photo John Wronn: 25.

© Khashayar Naimanan: 140.

Emmanuelle and Jérôme de Noirmont. Photo Mathieu Ferrier: 139 (top right).

Private Collection, USA: 51 (top right); 116 (bottom); photo Erik and Petra Hesmerg: 37, 44–45, 111 (top), 123 (bottom right and left).

Rosenthal AG Creative Center Selb: 178 (left).

Tim Simpson: 156 (bottom right).

Photo Stedelijk Museum / Erik and Petra Hesmerg: 18 (left), 23 (left center).

Stedelijk Museum, Amsterdam. Photo Stedelijk Museum / Erik and Petra Hesmerg: 14 (left), 23 (top and bottom left).

Stedelijk Museum, Amsterdam. Photo Stedelijk Museum: 21 (right).

Photo Ruy Teixeira: 15 (left).

Noam Toran: 156 (bottom left).

Courtesy Treadway Gallery: 22 (right).

Troika 2008: 148 (top left).

Archive Alexander von Vegesack: 34 (bottom), 39, 47 (top right, bottom center), 51 (bottom left and right), 56 (bottom right), 57 (bottom right), 77, 78 (left), 80 (top right).

Vitra Design Museum, Weil am Rhein, Germany: 18 (left), 22 (left), 38 (left), 40, 47 (bottom left, bottom right), 56 (top), 76, 96 (center).

Vitra, Switzerland: 27 (center and right), 41 (left), 82 (right), 88 (overlay), 89 (center), Dominic Wilcox Studio: 156 (top left).

Ben Wilson: 148 (top right).